R. A.
TORREY

R. A. TORREY

BAKER BOOK HOUSE
Grand Rapids, Michigan 49506

Copyright 1954 by
Fleming H. Revell Company

Reprinted 1968 by Baker Book House
under the title,
The Treasury of R. A. Torrey

Mass market paperback edition
issued 1982 by Baker Book House

ISBN: 0-8010-8865-8

PHOTOLITHOPRINTED BY CUSHING - MALLOY, INC.
ANN ARBOR, MICHIGAN, UNITED STATES OF AMERICA

Contents

Introduction

Dr. Reuben A. Torrey
Flaming Evangelist and Spirit-filled Writer

Dr. Reuben A. Torrey was one of the great evangelists of the Christian centuries—a companion in the timeless apostleship of Martin Luther, John Wesley, Charles G. Finney and Dwight L. Moody. Like his predecessors, he was a chosen vessel, called and empowered of the Spirit of God. Thousands who owe their salvation to him will recall how, half a century ago, the Torrey-Alexander meetings stirred and thrilled the Christian world and how, in a three-years' evangelistic tour of Australia, New Zealand, India, and Great Britain, more than 100,000 people publicly confessed Christ as their personal Saviour.

Dr. Torrey's teammate in revival meetings, the smiling and magnetic Gospel singer, Charles W. Alexander, would "warm up" the great choirs and audiences; then Dr. Torrey would take the rostrum and begin to speak. None could mistake his passion and earnestness; few could remain unconvinced by the logical clearness with which he presented the Gospel message. To him every sinner was an involuntary client for whose soul he must do battle.

The evangelist's presence on the platform was impressive. His large, well-built frame, his piercing eyes, his white hair and beard, his powerful voice, and his magnetic appeal combined to create an atmosphere of religious fervor that has not yet died away among those who heard him. So conviction of sin came to his hearers and the way of salvation was made plain.

Dr. Torrey's faith was like the faith of those of immemorial record in the 11th chapter of the Epistle to the Hebrews. I shall never forget hearing him tell his audiences of how he had struggled for his faith. At first, it was like a man trying to lift himself up by his own bootstraps; later, however, he discovered the secret of the faith from which he never faltered—the faith that "cometh by hearing and hearing by the word of God." Then was his soul so steeped in trust in divine revelation that he was able to lead multitudes in many lands to the same refuge he had found for himself.

I was in religious journalism in Chicago at the time of the Torrey-Alexander revival meetings in Australia and Great Britain, and was invited to go to Great Britain to write up the great meetings there for the religious press. When I arrived in England, the meetings were being held in a large drill hall in Bolton, where the two evangelists held the people in the thrall of eloquence and song. Then I witnessed the great meetings in Liverpool, in London, and in Cardiff, Wales. Everywhere the story was the same. I am convinced that it was the Torrey-Alexander meetings in Cardiff that kindled the flame of the great Welsh Revival.

Dr. Torrey once told me the secret of the spiritual awakening that accompanied their meetings in England, Scotland, Ireland, and Wales. He said, "Prayer was the secret of the power in the meetings. Twenty thousand people banded together in prayer groups throughout Great Britain to pray for us and for the meetings, in addition to which there was intensive private prayer in each city we visited." That was the secret of the outpouring of God's spirit that brought religious awakening to the British Isles.

Dr. Torrey was not only pastor of the Moody Church, Chicago, and superintendent of the Moody Bible Institute and a flaming evangelist; he also was a prolific writer who brought to the printed page the same eloquent zeal that characterized his public utterance. Thus, by voice and pen, he gathered in a great harvest for his Lord.

GEORGE T. B. DAVIS

Philadelphia, Pa.

R. A. TORREY

I. Beginning Right

THERE is nothing more important in the Christian life than
beginning right. If we begin right, we can go on right. If
we begin wrong, the whole life that follows is likely to be
wrong. If anyone who reads these pages has begun wrong,
it is a very simple matter to begin over again and begin
right. What the right beginning in the Christian life is we
are told in John 1:12, "But as many as received him, to
them gave he power to become the sons of God, even to
them that believe on his name." The right way to begin the
Christian life is by receiving Jesus Christ. To anyone who
receives Him, He at once gives power to become a child of
God. If the reader of this book should be the wickedest man
on earth and should at this moment receive Jesus Christ,
that very instant he would become a child of God. God
says so in the most unqualified way in the verse quoted
above. No one can become a child of God in any other
way. No man, no matter how carefully he has been reared,
no matter how well he has been sheltered from the vices
and evils of this world, is a child of God until he receives
Jesus Christ. We are "sons of God through faith in Christ
Jesus" (Gal. 3:26, R.V.), and in no other way.

What does it mean to receive Jesus Christ? It means to
take Christ to be to yourself all that God offers Him to be
to everybody. Jesus Christ is God's gift. "For God so loved
the world that He gave his only begotten Son, that whoso-

13

ever believeth in him should not perish but have everlasting life" (John 3:16). Some accept this wondrous gift of God. Everyone who does accept this gift becomes a child of God. Many others refuse this wondrous gift of God, and everyone who refuses this gift of God perishes. He is condemned already. "He that believeth on the Son is not condemned, but he that believeth not is condemned already, because he hath not believed in the name of the only begotten Son of God" (John 3:18).

What does God offer His Son to be to us?

1. First of all, God offers Jesus to us to be our sin-bearer. We have all sinned. There is not a man or woman or a boy or a girl who has not sinned (Rom. 3:22, 23). If any of us say that we have not sinned we are deceiving ourselves and giving the lie to God (I John 1:8, 10). Now, we must each of us bear our own sin or some one else must bear it in our place. If we were to bear our own sins, it would mean we must be banished forever from the presence of God, for God is holy. "God is light and in him is no darkness at all" (I John 1:5). But God Himself has provided another to bear our sins in our place, so that we should not need to bear them ourselves. This sin-bearer is God's own Son, Jesus Christ: "For he hath made him to be sin for us who knew no sin, that we might be made the righteousness of God in him" (II Cor. 5:21). When Jesus Christ died on the cross of Calvary He redeemed us from the curse of the law by being made a curse in our stead (Gal. 3:13). To receive Christ, then, is to believe this testimony of God about His Son, to believe that Jesus Christ did bear our sins in His own body on the cross (I Pet. 2:24), and to trust God to forgive all our sins because Jesus Christ has borne them in our place. "All we like sheep have gone astray; we have turned every one to his own way; and the Lord hath

laid on him the iniquity of us all" (Is. 53:6). Our own good works, past, present, or future, have nothing to do with the forgiveness of our sins. Our sins are forgiven, not because of any good works that we do; they are forgiven because of the atoning work of Christ on the cross of Calvary in our place. If we rest in this atoning work we shall do good works, but our good works will be the outcome of our being saved and the outcome of our believing on Christ as our sin-bearer. Our good works will not be the ground of our salvation, but the result of our salvation, and the proof of it. We must be very careful not to mix in our good works at all as the ground of salvation. We are forgiven, not because of Christ's death and our good works, but solely and entirely because of Christ's death. To see this clearly is the right beginning of the true Christian life.

2. God offers Jesus to us as our deliverer from the power of sin. Jesus not only died, He rose again. Today He is a living Saviour. He has all power in heaven and on earth (Matt. 28:18). He has power to keep the weakest sinner from falling (Jude 24). He is able to save not only from the uttermost, but "to the uttermost," all that come unto the Father through Him. ("Wherefore he is able to save to the uttermost them that draw near unto God through him, seeing that he ever liveth to make intercession for them." —Heb. 7:25, R.V.) "If the Son therefore shall make you free, ye shall be free indeed" (John 8:36). To receive Jesus is to believe this that God tells us in His Word about Him, to believe that He did rise from the dead, to believe that He does now live, to believe that He has power to keep us from falling, to believe that He has power to keep us from the power of sin day by day, and just trust Him to do it.

This is the secret of daily victory over sin. If we try to fight sin in our own strength, we are bound to fail. If we just look up to the risen Christ to keep us every day and every hour, He will keep us. Through the crucified Christ we get deliverance from the guilt of sin, our sins are all blotted out, we are free from all condemnation; but it is through the risen Christ that we get daily victory over the power of sin. Some receive Christ as a sin-bearer and thus find pardon, but do not get beyond that, and so their life is one of daily failure. Others receive Him as their risen Saviour also, and thus enter into an experience of victory over sin. To begin right we must take Him not only as our sin-bearer, and thus find pardon; but we must also take Him as our risen Saviour, our Deliverer from the power of sin, our Keeper, and thus find daily victory over sin.

3. But God offers Jesus to us, not only as our sin-bearer and our Deliverer from the power of sin, but also as our Lord and King. We read in Acts 2:36, "Let all the house of Israel know assuredly, that God hath made that same Jesus, whom ye have crucified, both Lord and Christ." Lord means Divine Master, and Christ means anointed King. To receive Jesus is to take Him as our Divine Master, as the One to whom we yield the absolute confidence of our intellects, the One whose word we believe absolutely, the One whom we will believe, though many of the wisest of men may question or deny the truth of His teachings; and as our King to whom we gladly yield the absolute control of our lives, so that the question from this time on is never going to be, What would I like to do or what do others tell me to do, or what do others do? but *What would my King Jesus have me do?* A right

beginning involves an unconditional surrender to the Lordship and Kingship of Jesus.

The failure to realize that Jesus is Lord and King, as well as Saviour, has led to many a false start in the Christian life. We begin with Him as our Saviour, as our sin-bearer and our Deliverer from the power of sin, but we must not end with Him merely as Saviour; we must know Him as Lord and King. There is nothing more important in a right beginning of the Christian life than an unconditional surrender, both of the thoughts and the conduct, to Jesus. Say from your heart and say it again and again, "All for Jesus." Many fail because they shrink back from this entire surrender. They wish to serve Jesus with half their heart, and part of themselves, and part of their possessions. To hold back anything from Jesus means a wretched life of stumbling and failure.

The life of entire surrender is a joyous life all along the way. If you have never done it before, go alone with God today; get down on your knees, and say, "All for Jesus," and mean it. Say it very earnestly; say it from the bottom of your heart. Stay on your knees until you realize what it means and what you are doing. It is a wondrous step forward when one really takes it. If you have taken it already, take it again, take it often. It always has fresh meaning and brings fresh blessedness. In this absolute surrender is found the key to the truth. Doubts rapidly disappear for one who surrenders all (John 7:17). In this absolute surrender is found the secret of power in prayer (I John 3:22). In this absolute surrender is found the supreme condition of receiving the Holy Ghost (Acts 5:32).

Taking Christ as your Lord and King involves obedience to His will, so far as you know it, in each smallest detail of life. There are those who tell us that they have taken Christ as their Lord and King who at the same time are disobeying Him daily in business, in domestic life, in social life, and in personal conduct. Such persons are deceiving themselves. You have not taken Jesus as your Lord and King if you are not striving to obey Him in everything each day. He Himself says, "Why call ye me Lord, Lord! and do not the things that I say?" (Luke 6:46).

To sum it all up, the right way to begin the Christian life is to accept Jesus Christ as your sin-bearer and to trust God to forgive your sins because Jesus Christ died in your place; to accept Him as your risen Saviour who ever lives to make intercession for you, and who has all power to keep you, and to trust Him to keep you from day to day; and to accept Him as your Lord and King to whom you surrender the absolute control of your thoughts and of your life. This is the right beginning, the only right beginning of the Christian life. If you have made this beginning, all that follows will be comparatively easy. If you have not made this beginning, make it now.

II. Looking Unto Jesus

IF WE ARE to run with patience the race that is set before us, we must always keep looking unto Jesus (Heb. 12:1-3). One of the simplest and yet one of the mightiest secrets of abiding joy and victory is to never lose sight of Jesus.

1. First of all, we must keep looking at Jesus as the ground of our acceptance before God. Over and over again, Satan will make an attempt to discourage us by bringing up our sins and failures and thus try to convince us that we are not children of God, or not saved. If he succeeds in getting us to keep looking at and brooding over our sins, he will soon get us discouraged, and discouragement means failure. But if we will keep looking at what God looks at, the death of Jesus Christ in our place that completely atones for every sin that we ever committed, we will never be discouraged because of the greatest of our sins. We shall see that while our sins are great, very great, indeed they have all been atoned for. Every time Satan brings up one of our sins, we shall see that Jesus Christ has redeemed us from its curse by being made a curse in our place (Gal. 3:13). We shall see that while in ourselves we are full of unrighteousness, nevertheless in Christ we are made the righteousness of God, because Christ was made to be sin in our place (II Cor. 5:21). We will see that every sin that Satan taunts us about has been

borne and settled forever (I Pet. 2:24; Is. 53:6). We shall always be able to sing,

> Jesus paid my debt,
>   All the debt I owe;
> Sin had left a crimson stain,
>   He washed it white as snow.

If you are this moment troubled about any sin that you have ever committed, either in the past or in the present, just look at Jesus on the cross; believe what God tells you about Him, that this sin which troubles you was laid upon Him (Is. 53:6). Thank God that the sin is all settled, be full of gratitude to Jesus, who bore it in your place, and trouble about it no more. It is an act of base ingratitude to God to brood over sins that He in His infinite love has canceled. Keep looking at Christ on the cross and walk always in the sunlight of God's favor. This favor of God has been purchased for you at great cost. Gratitude demands that you should always believe in it and walk in the light of it.

2. In the second place, we must keep looking at Jesus as our risen Saviour, who has all power in heaven and on earth and is able to keep us every day and every hour. Are you tempted to do some wrong at this moment? If you are, remember that Jesus rose from the dead, remember that at this moment He is living at the right hand of God in the glory; remember that He has all power in heaven and on earth, and that, therefore, He can give you victory right now. Believe what God tells you in His Word, that Jesus has power to save you this moment "to the uttermost" (Heb. 7:25). Believe that He has power to give you victory over this sin that now besets you. Ask Him to give you victory; expect Him to do it. In this way,

by looking unto the risen Christ for victory, you may have victory over sin every day, every hour, every moment. "Remember Jesus Christ risen from the dead" (II Tim. 2:8, R.V.).

God has called every one of us to a victorious life, and the secret of this victorious life is always looking to the risen Christ for victory. Through looking to Christ crucified we obtain pardon and enjoy peace. Through looking to the risen Christ we obtain present victory over the power of sin. If you have lost sight of the risen Christ and have yielded to temptation, confess your sin and know that it is forgiven because God says so (I John 1:9), and look to Jesus, the risen One, again to give you victory now, and keep looking to Him.

3. In the third place, we must keep looking to Jesus as the One whom we should follow in our daily conduct. Our Lord Jesus says to us, His disciples today, as He said to His early disciples, "Follow me." The whole secret of true Christian conduct can be summed up in these two words "Follow me." "He that saith he abideth in him ought himself so to walk, even as he walked" (I John 2:6). One of the commonest causes of failure in Christian life is found in the attempt to follow some good man whom we greatly admire. No man and no woman, no matter how good, can be safely followed. If we follow any man or woman, we are bound to go astray. There has been but one absolutely perfect Man on this earth— the Man Christ Jesus. If we try to follow any other man we are surer to imitate his faults than his excellencies. Look to Jesus and Jesus only as your Guide.

If at any time you are in any perplexity as to what to do, simply ask the question, What would Jesus do? Ask God by His Holy Spirit to show you what Jesus would do. Study your Bible to find out what Jesus did do, and follow Him. Even though no one else seems to be following Jesus, be sure that you follow Him. Do not spend your time or thought in criticizing others because they do not follow Jesus. See that you follow Him yourself. When you are wasting your time criticizing others for not following Jesus, Jesus is always saying to you, "What is that to thee? Follow *thou* me" (John 21:22). The question for you is not what following Jesus may involve for other people. The question is, What does following Jesus mean for you?

This is the really simple life, the life of simply following Jesus. Many perplexing questions will come to you, but the most perplexing question will soon become as clear as day if you determine with all your heart to follow Jesus in everything. Satan will always be ready to whisper to you, "Such and such a good man does it," but all you need to do is to answer, "It matters not to me what this or that man may do or not do. The only question to me is, What would Jesus do?" There is wonderful freedom in this life of simply following Jesus. This path is straight and plain. But the path of him who tries to shape his conduct by observing the conduct of others is full of twists and turns and pitfalls. Keep looking at Jesus. Follow on trustingly where He leads. This is the path of the just, which shineth more and more unto the perfect day (Prov. 4:18). He is the Light of the world, any one who follows Him shall not walk in darkness, but shall have the light of life all along the way (John 8:12).

III. The Personality of the
Holy Spirit

Before one can correctly understand the work of the
Holy Spirit, he must first of all know the Spirit himself.
A frequent source of error and fanaticism about the work
of the Holy Spirit is the attempt to study and understand
His work without, first of all, coming to know Him as a
person.

It is of the highest importance from the standpoint of
worship that we decide whether the Holy Spirit is a Divine
Person, worthy to receive our adoration, our faith, our
love, and our entire surrender to Himself, or whether it
is simply an influence emanating from God or a power or
an illumination that God imparts to us. If the Holy Spirit
is a person, and a Divine Person, and we do not know Him
as such, then we are robbing a Divine Being of the wor-
ship and the faith and the love and the surrender to Him-
self which are His due.

It is also of the highest importance from the practical
standpoint that we decide whether the Holy Spirit is
merely some mysterious and wonderful power that we in
our weakness and ignorance are, somehow, to get hold of
and use, or whether the Holy Spirit is a real Person, in-
finitely holy, infinitely wise, infinitely mighty and infi-
nitely tender, who is to get hold of and use us. The former

23

conception is utterly heathenish, not essentially different from the thought of the African fetish worshiper who has his god whom he uses. The latter conception is sublime and Christian. If we think of the Holy Spirit, as so many do, as merely a power of influence, our constant thought will be, "How can I get more of the Holy Spirit?" But if we think of Him in the Biblical way as a Divine Person, our thought will rather be, "How can the Holy Spirit have more of me?" The conception of the Holy Spirit as a Divine influence or power that somehow, we are to get hold of and use, leads to self-exaltation and self-sufficiency. One who so thinks of the Holy Spirit and who at the same time imagines that he has received the Holy Spirit will almost inevitably be full of spiritual pride and strut about as if he belonged to some superior order of Christians. One frequently hears such persons say, "I am a Holy Ghost man," or "I am a Holy Ghost woman." But if we once grasp the thought that the Holy Spirit is a Divine Person of infinite majesty, glory and holiness and power, who in marvelous condescension has come into our hearts to make His abode there and take possession of our lives and make use of them, it will put us in the dust and keep us in the dust. I can think of no thought more humbling or more overwhelming than the thought that a person of Divine majesty and glory dwells in my heart and is ready to use even me.

It is of the highest importance from the standpoint of experience that we know the Holy Spirit as a person. Thousands and tens of thousands of men and women can testify to the blessing that has come into their own lives as they have come to know the Holy Spirit, not merely as a gracious influence (emanating, it is true, from God), but as a real Person, just as real as Jesus Christ Himself, an ever-present, loving Friend and mighty Helper, who is not only always by their side but dwells in their heart every day and every hour, and who is ready to undertake for them in every emergency of life. Thousands of ministers, Christian workers and Christians in the humblest spheres of life have spoken to me, or written to me, of the complete transformation of their Christian experience that came to them when they grasped the thought (not merely in a theological, but in an experimental way) that the Holy Spirit was a Person, and consequently came to know Him.

There are at least four distinct lines of proof in the Bible that the Holy Spirit is a person.

1. All the distinctive characteristics of personality are ascribed to the Holy Spirit in the Bible.

What are the distinctive characteristics, or marks, of personality? Knowledge, feeling, or emotion, and will. Any entity that thinks and feels and wills is a person. When we say that the Holy Spirit is a person, there are those who understand us to mean that the Holy Spirit has hands and feet and eyes and ears and mouth, and so on, but these are not the characteristics of personality but of corporeity. All of these characteristics or marks of personality are repeatedly ascribed to the Holy Spirit in the Old and New Testaments. We read in I Corinthians 2:10, 11, "But God hath revealed them unto us by his Spirit: for the Spirit searcheth all things, yea, the deep things of God. For what man knoweth the things of a man, save the spirit of man which is in him? even so the things of God knoweth no man, but the Spirit of God." Here knowledge is ascribed to the Holy Spirit. We are clearly taught that the Holy Spirit is not merely an influence that illuminates our minds to comprehend the truth but a Being who Himself knows the truth.

In I Corinthians 12:11, we read, "But all these worketh that one and the selfsame Spirit, dividing to every man severally as he will." Here will is ascribed to the Spirit and we are taught that the Holy Spirit is not a power that we get hold of and use according to our will but a Person of sovereign majesty, who uses us according to His will. This distinction is of fundamental importance in getting into right relations with the Holy Spirit. It is at this very point that many honest seekers after power and efficiency in service go astray. They are reaching out after, and struggling to get, possession of some mysterious and mighty power that they can make use of in their work according to their own will. They will never get possession of the power they seek until they come to recognize that there is not some Divine power for them to get hold of and use in their blindness and ignorance, but that there is a Person, infinitely wise, as well as infinitely mighty, who is willing to take possession of them and use them according to His own perfect will. When we stop to think of it, we must rejoice that there is no Divine power that beings so ignorant as we are, so liable to err, can get hold of and use. How appalling might be the results if there were. But what a holy joy must come into our hearts when we grasp the thought that there is a Divine Person, One who never errs, who is willing to take possession of us and impart to us such gifts as He sees best and to use us according to His wise and loving will.

We read in Romans 8:27, "And he that searcheth the hearts knoweth what is the mind of the Spirit, because he maketh intercession for the saints according to the will of

God." In this passage mind is ascribed to the Holy Spirit. The Greek word translated "mind" is a comprehensive word, including the ideas of thought, feeling, and purpose. It is the same that is used in Romans 8:7, where we read that "the carnal mind is enmity against God: for it is not subject to the law of God, neither indeed can be." So, then, in this passage we have all the distinctive marks of personality ascribed to the Holy Spirit.

We find the personality of the Holy Spirit brought out in a most touching and suggestive way in Romans 15:30, "Now I beseech you, brethren, for the Lord Jesus Christ's sake, and for the love of the Spirit, that ye strive together with me in your prayers to God for me." Here we have "love" ascribed to the Holy Spirit. The reader would do well to stop and ponder those five words, "the love of the Spirit." We dwell often on the love of God the Father. It is the subject of our daily and constant thought. We dwell often on the love of Jesus Christ the Son. Who would think of calling himself a Christian who passed a day without meditating on the love of his Saviour, but how often have we meditated on "the love of the Spirit"? Each day of our lives, if we are living as Christians ought, we kneel down in the presence of God the Father and look up into His face and say, "I thank Thee, Father, for Thy great love that led Thee to give Thine only begotten Son to die on the cross of Calvary for me." Each day of our lives we also look up into the face of our Lord and Saviour, Jesus Christ, and say, "Oh, Thou glorious Lord and Saviour, Jesus, Thou Son of God, I thank Thee for Thy great love that led Thee not to count it a thing to be grasped to be on equality with God but to empty Thyself and, forsaking all the glory of heaven, come down to earth with all its shame and to take my sins upon

Thyself and die in my place on the cross of Calvary." But how often do we kneel and say to the Holy Spirit, "Oh, Thou eternal and infinite Spirit of God, I thank Thee for Thy great love that led Thee to come into this world of sin and darkness and to seek me out and to follow me so patiently until Thou didst bring me to see my utter ruin and need of a Saviour and to reveal to me my Lord and Saviour, Jesus Christ, as just the Saviour whom I need"? Yet we owe our salvation just as truly to the love of the Spirit as to the love of the Father and the love of the Son. If it had not been for the love of God the Father looking down on me in my utter ruin and providing a perfect atonement for me in the death of His own Son on the cross of Calvary, I would have been in hell today. If it had not been for the love of Jesus Christ, the eternal Word of God, looking on me in my utter ruin and in obedience to the Father, putting aside all the glory of heaven for all the shame of earth and taking my place, the place of the curse on the cross of Calvary and pouring out His life utterly for me, I would have been in hell today. If it had not been for the love of the Holy Spirit, sent by the Father in answer to the prayer of the Son (John 14:16), leading Him to seek me out in my utter blindness and ruin and to follow me day after day, week after week, and year after year, when I persistently turned a deaf ear to His pleadings, following me through paths of sin where it must have been agony for that holy One to go, until at last I listened and He opened my eyes to see my utter ruin and then revealed Jesus to me as just the Saviour that would meet my every need and then enabled me to receive this Jesus as my own Saviour; if it had not been for this patient, long-suffering, never-tiring, infinitely tender love of the Holy Spirit, I would have been in hell today. Oh, the Holy Spirit is not merely an influence or a power or an illumination, but is a Person just as real as God the Father or Jesus Christ His Son.

The personality of the Holy Spirit comes out in the Old Testament as truly as in the New, for we read in Nehemiah 9:20, "Thou gavest also thy good spirit to instruct them, and withheldest not thy manna from their mouth, and gavest them water for their thirst." Here both intelligence and goodness are ascribed to the Holy Spirit. There are some who tell us that while it is true the personality of the Holy Spirit is found in the New Testament, it is not found in the Old. But it is certainly found in this passage. As a matter of course, the doctrine of the personality of the Holy Spirit is not so fully developed in the Old Testament as in the New. But the doctrine is there.

There is perhaps no passage in the entire Bible in which the personality of the Holy Spirit comes out more tenderly and touchingly than in Ephesians 4:30, "And grieve not the Holy Spirit of God, whereby ye are sealed unto the day of redemption." Here grief is ascribed to the Holy Spirit. The Holy Spirit is not a blind, impersonal influence or power that comes into our lives to illuminate, sanctify, and empower them. No, He is immeasurably more than that, He is a holy Person, who comes to dwell in our hearts, One who sees clearly every act we perform, every word we speak, every thought we entertain, even the most fleeting fancy that is allowed to pass through our minds; and if there is anything in act, or word or deed that is impure, unholy, unkind, selfish, mean, petty or untrue, this infinitely holy One is deeply grieved by it. I know of no thought that will help one more than this to lead a holy life and to walk softly in the presence of the holy One. How often a young man is kept back from yielding to the temptations that surround young manhood by the thought that if he should yield to the temptation that now assails him, his holy mother might hear of it and would be grieved by it beyond expression. How often some young man has had his hand on the door of some place of sin that he is about to enter and the thought has come to him, "If I should enter there, my mother might hear of it and it would nearly kill her," and he has turned his back on that door and gone away to lead a pure life, that he might not grieve his mother. But there is One who is holier than any mother, One who is more sensitive against sin than the purest woman who ever walked this earth, and who loves us as even no mother ever loved. This One dwells in our hearts, if we are really Christians, and He sees every act we do by day or under cover of the night; He hears every word we utter in public or in private; He sees every thought we entertain, He beholds every fancy and imagination that is permitted even a momentary lodgment in our mind, and if there is anything unholy, impure, selfish, mean, petty, unkind, harsh, unjust, or in any wise evil in act or word or thought or fancy, He is grieved by it. If we will allow those words, "Grieve not the Holy Spirit of God," to sink into our hearts and become the motto of our lives they will keep us from many a sin. How often some thought or fancy has knocked for an entrance into my own mind and was about to find entertainment when the thought has come, "The Holy Spirit sees that thought and will be grieved by it," and that thought has gone.

2. Many acts that only a Person can perform are ascribed to the Holy Spirit.

If we deny the personality of the Holy Spirit, many

passages of Scripture become meaningless and absurd. For example, we read in I Corinthians 2:10, "But God hath revealed them unto us by his Spirit: for the Spirit searcheth all things, yea, the deep things of God." This passage sets before us the Holy Spirit, not merely as an illumination whereby we are enabled to grasp the deep things of God, but a Person who Himself searches the deep things of God and then reveals to us the precious discoveries which He has made.

We read in Revelation 2:7, "He that hath an ear, let him hear what the Spirit saith unto the churches, To him that overcometh will I give to eat of the tree of life, which is in the midst of the paradise of God." Here the Holy Spirit is set before us, not merely as an impersonal enlightenment that comes to our mind but as a Person who speaks and out of the depths of His own wisdom whispers into the ear of His listening servant the precious truth of God.

In Galatians 4:6, we read, "And because ye are sons, God hath sent forth the Spirit of his Son into your hearts, crying, Abba, Father." Here the Holy Spirit is represented as crying out in the heart of the individual believer. Not merely a Divine influence producing in our own hearts the assurance of our sonship, but one who cries out in our hearts, who bears witness together with our spirit that we are sons of God. (See also Rom. 8:16.)

The Holy Spirit is also represented in the Scripture as one who prays. We read in Romans 8:26, R.V., "And in like manner the Spirit also helpeth our infirmity; for we know not how to pray as we ought; but the Spirit himself maketh intercession for us with groanings which cannot be uttered." It is plain from this passage that the Holy Spirit is not merely an influence that moves us to pray, not merely an illumination that teaches us how to pray, but a Person who Himself prays in and through us. There is wondrous comfort in the thought that every true believer has two Divine Persons praying for him, Jesus Christ, the Son who was once on this earth, who knows all about our temptations, who can be touched with the feeling of our infirmities and who is now ascended to the right hand of the Father and in that place of authority and power ever lives to make intercession for us (Heb. 7:25; I John 2:1); and another Person, just as Divine as the Son, who walks by our side each day, yes, who dwells in the innermost depths of our being and knows our needs, even as we do not know them ourselves, and from these depths makes intercession to the Father for us. The position of the believer is indeed one of perfect security with these two Divine Persons praying for him.

We read again in John 15:26, "But when the Comforter is come, whom I will send unto you from the Father, even the Spirit of truth, which proceedeth from the Father, he shall testify of me." Here the Holy Spirit is set before us as a Person who gives His testimony to Jesus Christ, not merely as an illumination that enables the believer to testify of Christ, but as a Person who Himself testifies; and a clear distinction is drawn in this and the following verse between the testimony of the Holy Spirit and the testimony of the believer to whom He has borne His witness, for we read in the next verse, "And ye also shall bear witness, because ye have been with me from the beginning." So there are two witnesses, the Holy Spirit bearing witness to the believer, and the believer bearing witness to the world.

The Holy Spirit is also spoken of as a teacher. We read in John 14:26, "But the Comforter, which is the Holy Ghost, whom the Father will send in my name, he shall teach you all things, and bring all things to your remembrance, whatsoever I have said unto you." And in a similar way, we read in John 16:12-14, "I have yet many things to say unto you, but ye cannot bear them now. Howbeit when he, the Spirit of truth, is come, he will guide you into all truth: for he shall not speak of himself; but whatsoever he shall hear, that shall he speak: and he will show you things to come. He shall glorify me: for he shall receive of mine, and shall show it unto you." And in the Old Testament, Nehemiah 9:20, "Thou gavest also thy good Spirit to instruct them." In all these passages it is perfectly clear that the Holy Spirit is not a mere illumination that enables us to apprehend the truth, but a Person who comes to us to teach us day by day the truth of God. It is the privilege of the humblest believer in Jesus Christ, not merely to have his mind illumined to comprehend the truth of God, but to have a Divine Teacher to teach him daily the truth he needs to know (cf. I John 2:20, 27). The Holy Spirit is also represented as the Leader and Guide of the children of God. We read in Romans 8:14, "For as many as are led by the Spirit of God they are the sons of God." He is not merely an influence that enables us to see the way that God would have us go, nor merely a power that gives us strength to go that way, but a Person who takes us by the hand and gently leads us on in the paths in which God would have us walk.

The Holy Spirit is also represented as a Person who has authority to command men in their service of Jesus Christ. We read of the Apostle Paul and his companions in Acts 16:6, 7, "Now when they had gone throughout Phrygia and the region of Galatia, and were forbidden of the Holy Ghost to preach the word in Asia, after they were come to Mysia, they assayed to go into Bithynia: but the Spirit suffered them not." Here it is a Person who takes the direction of the conduct of Paul and his companions and a Person whose authority they recognize and to whom they instantly submit.

Further still than this, the Holy Spirit is represented as the One who is the supreme authority in the church, who calls men to work and appoints them to office. We read in Acts 13:2, "As they ministered to the Lord, and fasted, the Holy Ghost said, Separate me Barnabas and Saul for the work where unto I have called them." And in Acts 20:28, "Take heed therefore unto yourselves, and to all the flock, over the which the Holy Ghost hath made you overseers, to feed the church of God, which he hath purchased with his own blood." There can be no doubt to a candid seeker after truth that it is a Person, and a person of Divine majesty and sovereignty, who is here set before us.

From all the passages here quoted, it is evident that many acts that only a person can perform are ascribed to the Holy Spirit.

3. An office is predicated of the Holy Spirit that can be predicated only of a person.

Our Saviour says in John 14:16, 17, "And I will pray the Father, and he shall give you another Comforter, that he may abide with you forever; even the Spirit of truth: whom the world cannot receive, because it seeth him not, neither knoweth him: but ye know him; for he dwelleth with you, and shall be in you." Our Lord had announced to the disciples that He was about to leave them. An awful sense of desolation took possession of them. Sorrow filled their hearts (John 16:6) at the contemplation of their loneliness and absolute helplessness when Jesus should thus leave them alone. To comfort them the Lord tells them that they shall not be left alone, that in leaving them He was going to the Father and that He would pray the Father, who would give them another Comforter to take the place of Himself during His absence. Is it possible that Jesus Christ could have used such language if the other Comforter who was coming to take His place was only an impersonal influence or power? Still more, is it possible that Jesus could have said as He did in John 16:7, "Nevertheless I tell you the truth: It is expedient for you that I go away: for if I go not away, the Comforter will not come unto you; but if I depart, I will send him unto you," if this Comforter whom He was to send was simply an impersonal influence or power? No, one Divine Person was going, another Person just as Divine was coming to take His place, and it was expedient for the disciples that the One go to represent them before the Father, for another just as Divine and sufficient was coming to take His place. This promise of our Lord and Saviour of the coming of the other Comforter and of His abiding with us is the greatest and best of all for the present dispensation. This is the promise of the Father (Acts 1:4), the promise of promises. We shall take it up again when we come to study the names of the Holy Spirit.

4. A treatment is predicated of the Holy Spirit that could be predicated only of a Person.

We read in Isaiah 63:10, R.V., "But they rebelled and grieved his Holy Spirit: therefore he was turned to be their enemy, and he fought against them." Here we are told that the Holy Spirit is rebelled against and grieved (cf. Eph. 4:30). Only a person can be rebelled against and only a person of authority. Only a person can be grieved. You cannot grieve a mere influence or power.

In Hebrews 10:29, we read, "Of how much sorer punishment, suppose ye, shall he be thought worthy, who hath trodden underfoot the Son of God, and hath counted the blood of the covenant, wherewith he was sanctified, an unholy thing, and hath done despite unto the Spirit of grace?" Here we are told that the Holy Spirit is "done despite unto" ("treated with contumely"—Thayer's Greek-English Lexicon of the New Testament). There is but one kind of entity in the universe that can be treated with contumely (or insulted) and that is a person. It is absurd to think of treating an influence or a power or any kind of being except a person with contumely. We read again in Acts 5:3, "But Peter said, Ananias, why hath Satan filled thine heart to lie to the Holy Ghost, and to keep back part of the price of the land?" Here we have the Holy Spirit represented as one who can be lied to. One cannot lie to anything but a person.

In Matthew 12:31, 32, we read, "Wherefore I say unto you, All manner of sin and blasphemy shall be forgiven unto men: but the blasphemy against the Holy Ghost shall not be forgiven unto men. And whosoever speaketh a word against the Son of man, it shall be forgiven him: but whosoever speaketh against the Holy Ghost, it shall not be forgiven him, neither in this world, neither in the world to come." Here we are told that the Holy Spirit is blasphemed against. It is impossible to blaspheme anything but a person. If the Holy Spirit is not a person, it certainly cannot be a more serious and decisive sin to blaspheme Him than it is to blaspheme the Son of man, our Lord and Saviour, Jesus Christ Himself.

Here, then, we have four distinctive and decisive lines of proof that the Holy Spirit is a Person. Theoretically most of us believe this, but do we, in our real thought of

Him and in our practical attitude toward Him, treat Him as if He were indeed a Person? At the close of an address on the Personality of the Holy Spirit at a Bible conference some years ago, one who had been a church member many years, a member of one of the most orthodox of our modern denominations, said to me, "I never thought of It before as a Person." Doubtless this Christian woman had often sung:

> Praise God from whom all blessings flow,
> Praise Him all creatures here below,
> Praise Him above, ye heavenly host,
> Praise Father, Son and Holy Ghost.

Doubtless she had often sung:

Glory be to the Father, and to the Son, and to the Holy Ghost,
As it was in the beginning, is now, and ever shall be,
World without end, Amen.

But it is one thing to sing words; it is quite another thing to realize the meaning of what we sing. If this Christian woman had been questioned in regard to her doctrine, she would doubtless have said that she believed that there were three Persons in the Godhead—Father, Son, and Holy Spirit—but a theological confession is one thing, a practical realization of the truth we confess is quite another. So the question is altogether necessary, no matter how orthodox you may be in your creedal statements, Do you regard the Holy Spirit as indeed as real a Person as Jesus Christ, as loving and wise and strong, as worthy of your confidence and love and surrender as Jesus Christ Himself? The Holy Spirit came into this world to be to the disciples of our Lord after His departure, and to us, what Jesus Christ had been to them during the days of His personal companionship with them (John 14:16, 17). Is He that to you? Do you know Him? Every week in your life you hear the apostolic benediction, "The grace of the Lord Jesus Christ and the love of God and the communion of the Holy Ghost be with you all" (II Cor. 13:14), and while you hear it, do you take in the significance of it? Do you know the communion of the Holy Ghost? The fellowship of the Holy Ghost? The partnership of the Holy Ghost? The comradeship of the Holy Ghost? The intimate personal friendship of the Holy Ghost? Herein lies the whole secret of a real Christian life, a life of liberty and joy and power and fullness. To have as one's ever-present Friend, and to be conscious that one has as his ever-present Friend, the Holy Spirit, and to surrender one's life in all its departments entirely to His control, this is true Christian living. The doctrine of the Personality of the Holy Spirit is as distinctive of the religion that Jesus taught as the doctrines of the Deity and the atonement of Jesus Christ Himself. But it is not enough to believe the doctrine—one must know the Holy Spirit Himself. The whole purpose of this chapter (God help me to say it reverently) is to introduce you to my Friend, the Holy Spirit.

IV. The Power of Prayer

Ye have not, because ye ask not.
JAMES 4:2.

I BRING you a message from God contained in seven short words. Six of the seven words are monosyllables, and the remaining word has but two syllables and is one of the most familiar and most easily understood words in the English language. Yet there is so much in these seven short, simple words that they have transformed many a life and brought many an inefficient worker into a place of great power.

I spoke on these seven words some years ago at a Bible conference in Central New York. Some months after the conference I received a letter from the man who had presided at the conference, one of the best-known ministers of the Gospel in America. He wrote me: "I have been unable to get away from the seven words upon which you spoke at Lake Keuka; they have been with me day and night. They have transformed my ideas, transformed my methods, transformed my life, and, I think I have a right to add, transformed my ministry." Since he wrote those words the man has been the pastor of what is probably the most widely known of any evangelical church in the world. I trust that the words may sink into some of your hearts today as they sank into his on that occasion, and that some of you will be able to say in future months and years, "I have been unable to get away from those seven words, they have been with me day and night. They have transformed my ideas, transformed my methods, transformed my life, and transformed my service for God."

You will find these seven words in James 4:2, the seven closing words of the verse, "Ye have not, *because ye ask not.*"

These seven words contain the secret of the poverty and powerlessness of the average Christian, of the average minister, and of the average church. "Why is it," many a Christian is asking, "that I make such poor progress in my Christian life? Why do I have so little victory over sin? Why do I win so few souls to Christ? Why do I grow so slowly into the likeness of my Lord and Saviour Jesus Christ?" And God answers in the words of our text —"Neglect of prayer. You have not, because you ask not."

"Why is it," many a minister is asking, "that I see so little fruit from my ministry? Why are there so few conversions? Why does my church grow so slowly? Why are the members of my church so little helped by my ministry, and built up so little in Christian knowledge and life?" And again God replies: "Neglect of prayer. You have not, because you ask not."

"Why is it," both ministers and churches are asking, "that the Church of Jesus Christ is making such slow progress in the world today? Why does it make so little headway against sin, against unbelief, against error in all its forms? Why does it have so little victory over the world, the flesh, and the devil? Why is the average church member living on such a low plane of Christian living?

Why does the Lord Jesus Christ get so little honor from the state of the Church today?" And, again, God replies: "Neglect of prayer. You have not, because you ask not."

When we read the only inspired church history that ever was written, the history of the Church in the days of the Apostles as it is recorded by Luke (under the inspiration of the Holy Spirit) in the Acts of the Apostles, what do we find? We find a story of constant victory, a story of perpetual progress. We read, for example, such statements as this in Acts 2:47: "The Lord added to the church daily those that were being saved," and such statements as this in Acts 4:4: "Many of them which heard the word believed; and the number of the men came to be about five thousand," and such statements as this in Acts 5:14: "And believers were the more added to the Lord, multitudes both of men and women."

And such statements as this in Acts 6:7: "And the word of God increased; and the number of the disciples multiplied in Jerusalem exceedingly; and a great company of the priests were obedient to the faith."

And so we go on, chapter after chapter, through the twenty-eight chapters of the book, and in every one of the twenty-seven chapters after the first we find the same note of victory. I once went through the Acts of the Apostles marking the note of victory in every chapter, and without one single exception the triumphant shout of victory rang out in every chapter. How different the history of the Church as here recorded is from the history of the Church of Jesus Christ today. Take, for example, that first statement, "The Lord added to the church daily [that is, every day, or, as the Revised Version puts it, "day by day"] those that were being saved." Why, nowadays if we have a revival once a year with an accession of fifty or sixty members and spend all the rest of the year slipping back to where we were before, we think we are doing pretty well. But in those days there was a revival all the time and accessions every day of those who not only "hit the trail" but "were [really] being saved."

Why this difference between the Early Church and the Church of Jesus Christ today? Someone will answer, "Because there is so much opposition today." Ah, but there was opposition in those days: most bitter, most determined, most relentless opposition, opposition in comparison with which that which you and I meet today is but child's play. But the Early Church went right on beating down all opposition, surmounting every obstacle, conquering every foe, always victorious, right on without a setback from Jerusalem to Rome, in the face of the most firmly entrenched and most mighty heathenism and unbelief. I repeat the question—"Why was it?" If you will turn to the chapters from which I have already quoted, you will get your answer.

Turn, for example, to the first chapter from which I quoted, Acts 2, and read the 42nd verse: "And they continued stedfastly in the apostles' teaching and fellowship, in the breaking of bread and the prayers." That is a picture, very brief but very suggestive, of the Early Church. *It was a praying church*. It was a church in which they prayed not merely occasionally, but in which they all "continued stedfastly . . . in the prayers." They all prayed, not a select few, but the whole membership of the church; and all prayed continuously with stedfast determination. "They gave themselves to prayer," as the same Greek word is translated in Acts 6:4. Now turn to the last chapter from which I quoted, the sixth chapter, verse 4, and you will get the rest of your answer. "We will give ourselves continually to prayer." That is a picture of the Apostolic ministry, it was a praying ministry, and a ministry that "gave themselves continually to prayer," or, to translate that Greek word as it is translated in the former passage (Acts 2:42), "They continued stedfastly in prayer." *A praying church and a praying ministry!* Ah, such a church and such a ministry can achieve anything that ought to be achieved. It will go steadily on beating down all opposition, surmounting every obstacle, conquering every foe, just as much today as it did in the days of the Apostles.

There is nothing else in which the church of today, and the ministry of today, or, to be more explicit, in which you and I, have departed more notably and more lamentably from apostolic precedent than in this matter of prayer. We do not live in a praying age. A very considerable proportion of the membership of our evangelical churches today do not believe even theoretically in prayer, that is, they do not believe in prayer as bringing anything to pass that would not have come to pass even if they had not prayed. They believe in prayer as having a beneficial "reflex influence," that is, as benefiting the person who prays, a sort of lifting yourself up by your spiritual boot-straps, but as for prayer bringing anything to pass that would not have come to pass if we had not prayed, they do not believe in it and many of them frankly say so, and even some of our "modern ministers" say so.

And with that part of our church membership that does believe in prayer theoretically—and, thank God, I believe it is still the vast majority in our evangelical churches—even they do not make the use of this mighty instrument that God has put into our hands that one would naturally ex-

pect. As I said, we do not live in a praying age. We live in
an age of hustle and bustle, of man's efforts and man's de-
termination, of man's confidence in himself and in his own
power to achieve things, an age of human organization,
and human machinery, and human push, and human schem-
ing, and human achievement, which in the things of God
means no real achievement at all. I think it would be per-
fectly safe to say that the Church of Christ was never in
all its history so fully and so skillfully and so thoroughly
and so perfectly organized as it is today. Our machinery is
wonderful, it is just perfect, but, alas, it is machinery with-
out power; and when things do not go right, instead of go-
ing to the real source of our failure, our neglect to depend
on God and to look to God for power, we glance around
to see if there is not some new organization we can get up,
some new wheel that we can add to our machinery. We
have altogether too many wheels already. What we need
is not so much some new organization, some new wheel,
but "the Spirit of the living creature in the wheels" we al-
ready possess.

I believe that the devil stands and looks at the church
today and laughs in his sleeve as he sees how its members
depend on their own scheming and powers of organization
and skillfully devised machinery. "Ha, ha," he laughs, "you
may have your Y.M.C.A.'s, and Y.W.C.A.'s, and your
W.C.T.U.'s, and Y.P.S.C.E.'s, and B.Y.P.U.'s, and your Boy
Scouts, and your costly church edifices, and your fifty-
thousand-dollar church organs, and your brilliant univer-
sity-bred preachers, and your high-priced choirs, and your
gifted sopranos, and altos, and tenors, and basses, and
your wonderful quartets; your immense Men's Bible
Classes, yes, and your Bible Conferences, and your Bible
Institutes, and your special evangelistic services, all you

please of them, but it does not in the least trouble me if only you will leave out of them the power of the Lord God Almighty sought and obtained by the earnest, persistent, believing prayer that will not take 'no' for an answer." But when the devil sees a man or woman who really believes in prayer, who knows how to pray, and who really does pray, and, above all, when he sees a whole church on its face before God in prayer, "he trembles" as much as he ever did, for he knows that his day in that church or community is at an end.

Prayer has as much power today, when men and women are themselves on praying ground and meeting the conditions of prevailing prayer, as it ever has had. God has not changed, and His ear is just as quick to hear the voice of real prayer and His hand is just as long and strong to save as they ever were. "Behold, the Lord's hand is not shortened, that it cannot save: neither his ear heavy, that it cannot hear." But "our iniquities" may "have separated between us and our God, and our sins" may "have hid his face from us, that he will not hear" (Is. 59:1, 2). Prayer is the key that unlocks all the storehouses of God's infinite grace and power. All that God is, and all that God has, is at the disposal of prayer. But we must use the key. Prayer can do anything that God can do, and as God can do anything, prayer is omnipotent. No one can stand against the man who knows how to pray and who meets all the conditions of prevailing prayer and who really prays. "The Lord God omnipotent" works for him and works through him.

I. Prayer Will Promote Our Personal Holiness as Nothing Else, Except the Study of the Word of God

But what, specifically, will prayer do? We have been dealing in generalities; let us come down to the definite and specific. The Word of God very plainly answers the question.

In the first place, prayer will promote our personal piety, our individual holiness, our individual growth into the likeness of Our Lord and Saviour Jesus Christ as almost nothing else, as nothing else but the study of the Word of God; and these two things, prayer and study of the Word of God, always go hand in hand, for there is not true prayer without study of the Word of God, and there is no true study of the Word of God without prayer.

Other things being equal, your growth and mine into the likeness of our Lord and Saviour Jesus Christ will be in exact proportion to the time and to the heart we put into prayer. Please note exactly what I say: "Your growth and mine into the likeness of our Lord and Saviour Jesus Christ will be in exact proportion to the time and to the heart we put into prayer." I put it in that way because there are many who put a great deal of time into praying but they put so little heart into their praying that they do very little praying in the long time they spend at it; while there are others who perhaps may not put so much time into praying but who put so much heart into their praying that they accomplish vastly more by their praying in a short time than the others accomplish by their praying a long time. God Himself has told us in Jeremiah 29:13: "And ye shall seek me, and find me, when ye shall search for me with all your heart."

We are told in the Word of God in Ephesians 1:3 that God hath blessed us with every spiritual blessing in the heavenly places in Christ. That is to say, that Jesus Christ, by His atoning death and by His resurrection and ascension to the right hand of the Father, has obtained for every believer in Jesus Christ every possible spiritual blessing.

There is no spiritual blessing that any believer enjoys that may not be yours. It belongs to you now, Christ purchased it by His atoning death, and God has provided it in Him. It is there for you; but it is your part to claim it, to put out your hand and take it, and God's appointed way of claiming blessings, or putting out your hand and appropriating to yourself the blessings that are procured for you by the atoning death of Jesus Christ, is by prayer. Prayer is the hand that takes to ourselves the blessings that God has already provided in His Son.

Go through your Bible and you will find it definitely stated that every conceivable spiritual blessing is obtained by prayer. For example, it is in answer to prayer, as we learn from Psalm 139:23, 24, that God searches us and knows our hearts, tries us and knows our thoughts, brings to light the sin that there is in us, and delivers us from it. It is in answer to prayer, as we learn from Psalm 19:12, 13, that we are cleansed from secret faults and God keeps us back from presumptuous sins. It is in answer to prayer, as we learn from the 14th verse of the same Psalm, that "the words of our mouth and the meditations of our heart are made acceptable in God's sight." It is in answer to prayer, as we learn from the 25th Psalm, verses 4 and 5, that God shows us His ways and teaches us His path, and guides us in His truth. It is in answer to prayer, as we learn from the prayer our Lord Himself taught us, that we are kept from temptation and delivered from the power of the wicked one (Matt. 6:13 R.V.). It is in answer to prayer, as we learn from Luke 11:13, that God gives us His Holy Spirit. And so we might go on through the whole catalogue of spiritual blessings, and we would find that every one is obtained by asking for it. Indeed, our Lord Himself said in Matthew 7:11: "If ye then, being evil, know how to give good gifts unto your children, how much more shall your Father which is in heaven give good things to them that ask him?"

One of the most instructive and suggestive passages in the entire Bible as showing the mighty power of prayer to transform us into the likeness of our Lord Jesus Himself, is found in II Corinthians 3:18, R.V.: "But we all, with unveiled face beholding as in a mirror [the English Revision reads better, "reflecting as a mirror"] the glory of the Lord, are transformed into the same image from glory to glory, even as from the Lord the Spirit." The thought is this, that the Lord is the sun, you and I mirrors, and just as a mischievous boy on a bright sunshiny day will catch the rays of the sun in a piece of broken looking-glass and reflect them into your eyes and mine with almost blinding power, so we as mirrors, when we commune with God, catch the rays of His moral glory and reflect them out on the world "from glory to glory," that is, each new time we commune with Him we catch something new of His glory and reflect it out on the world. You remember the story of Moses, not "folklore" as some would have us believe, but actual history, how he went up into the Mount and tarried alone for forty days with God, gazing on that ineffable glory, and caught so much of the glory in his own face that when he came down from the Mount, though he himself knew it not, his face so shone that he had to draw a veil over it to hide the blinding glory of it from his fellow Israelites. Even so we, going up into the Mount of prayer, away from the world, alone with God, and remaining long alone with God, catch the rays of His glory so that when we come down to our fellow men, it is not so much our faces that shine (though I do believe that sometimes even our faces shine), as our characters, with the glory that we have been beholding, and we reflect out on the world the moral glory of God from "glory to glory," each new time of communion with Him catching something new of His glory to reflect out on the world. Oh, here is the secret of becoming much like God—remaining long alone with God. If you won't stay long with Him you won't be much like Him.

One of the most remarkable men in Scotland's history was John Welch, son-in-law of John Knox, the great Scotch reformer, not so well known as his famous father-in-law but in some respects a far more remarkable man than John Knox himself. Most people have the idea that it was John Knox who prayed: "Give me Scotland or I die." It was not, it was John Welch, his son-in-law. John Welch put it on record before he died that he counted that day ill spent that he did not put seven or eight hours into secret prayer; and when John Welch came to die, an old Scotchman who had known him from his boyhood said of him, "John Welch was a type of Christ." Of course, that was an inaccurate use of language, but what the old Scotchman meant was that Jesus Christ had stamped the impress of His character on John Welch. When had Jesus Christ done it? In those seven or eight hours of daily communion with Himself. I do not suppose that God has called many of us, if any of us, to put seven or eight hours a day into prayer, but I am confident God has called most of us, if not every one of us, to put more time into prayer than we now do. That is one of the great secrets of holiness; indeed, the only way in which we can become really holy and continue holy.

Some years ago we often sang a hymn, "Take Time to be Holy." I wish we sang it more in these days. It takes time to be holy; one cannot be holy in a hurry, and much of the time that it takes to be holy must go into secret prayer. Some people express surprise that professing Christians today are so little like their Lord, but when I stop to think how little time the average Christian today puts into secret prayer the thing that astonishes me is, not that we are so little like the Lord, but that we are as much like the Lord as we are, when we take so little time for secret prayer.

II. Prayer Will Bring the Power of God into Our Work

But not only will prayer promote as almost nothing else our personal holiness, but prayer will also bring the power of God into our work. We read in Isaiah 40:31: "They that wait upon the Lord shall renew their strength; they shall mount up with wings as eagles; they shall run, and not be weary; and they shall walk [plod right along day after day, which is far harder than running or flying], and not faint."

It is the privilege of every child of God to have the power of God in his service. And the verse just quoted tells us how to obtain it, and that is by "waiting upon the Lord." Sometimes you will hear people stand up in meeting, not so frequently perhaps in these days as in former days, and say: "I am trying to serve God in my poor, weak way." Well, if you are trying to serve God in your poor, weak way, quit it: your duty is to serve God in His strong, triumphant way. But you say, "I have no natural ability"; then get supernatural ability. The religion of Jesus Christ is a supernatural religion from start to finish, and we should live our lives in supernatural power, the power of God through Jesus Christ, and we should perform our service with supernatural power, the power of God ministered by the Holy Spirit through Jesus Christ. You say, "I have no natural gifts." Then get supernatural gifts. The Holy Spirit is promised to every believer in order that he may obtain the supernatural gifts which qualify him for the particular service to which God calls him. "He [the Holy Spirit] divideth to each one [that is, to each and every believer] severally even as he will" (I Cor. 12:11). It is ours to have the power of God if only we will seek it by prayer, in any and every line of service to which God calls us.

Are you a mother or a father? Do you wish power from God to bring your own children up in the "nurture and admonition of the Lord"? God commands you to do it, and especially commands the father to do it. God says in Ephesians 6:4: "Ye fathers, provoke not your children to wrath: but bring them up in the nurture and admonition of the Lord."

Now, God never commands the impossible, and as He commands us fathers, and the mothers also, to bring our children up in the nurture and admonition of the Lord it is possible for us to do it. If any one of your children is not saved, the first blame lies at your own door. Paul said to the jailer in Philippi: "Believe on the Lord Jesus Christ, and thou shalt be saved, and thy house" (Acts 16:31).

Yes, it is the solemn duty of every father and mother to have every one of their children saved. But we can never accomplish it unless we are much in prayer to God for power to do it. In my first pastorate I had as a member of my church a most excellent Christian woman, but she had a little boy of six who was one of the most incorrigible youngsters I ever knew in my life. He was the terror of the community, the most difficult boy, I think, I ever knew. One Sunday, at the close of the morning service, his mother came to me and said: "You know ——" calling her boy by his first name. "Yes," I replied, "I know him." Everybody in town knew him. Then she said, "You know he is not a very good boy." "Yes," I replied, "I know he is not a very good boy." Indeed, that was a decidedly euphemistic way of putting it; in point of fact, he was the terror of the neighborhood. Then this heavy-hearted mother said, "What shall I do?" I replied, "Have you ever tried prayer?" "Why," she said, "of course I pray." "Oh," I said, "that is not what I mean. Have you ever asked God definitely to regenerate your boy and expected Him to do it?" "I do not think I have ever been as definite as that." "Well," I said, "you go right home and be just as definite as that." She went home, she was just as definite as that; and I think it was from that very day, certainly from that week, that the boy was a transformed boy and so began to grow up into fine young manhood.

Oh, mothers and fathers, it is your privilege to have every one of your children saved. But it costs something to have them saved. It costs your spending much time alone with God, to be much in prayer, and it costs also your making those sacrifices, and straightening out those things in your life that are wrong; it costs the fulfilling of the conditions of prevailing prayer. And if any of you have unsaved children, when you go home today get alone with God and ask God to show you what it is in your own life that is responsible for the present condition of your children, and straighten it out at once, and then get down alone before God and hold on to Him in earnest prayer for the definite conversion of each one of your children, and do not rest until, by prayer and by putting forth every effort, you know beyond question that every one of your children is definitely and positively converted and born again.

Are you a Sunday-school teacher? Do you wish to see every one of your Sunday-school pupils converted? That is primarily what you are a Sunday-school teacher for, not merely to teach Bible geography and Bible history, or even Bible doctrine, but to get the pupils in your class, one and all, saved. Do you want power from on high to enable you to save them? Ask God for it.

When Mr. Alexander and I were holding meetings in Sydney, Australia, the meetings were held in the Town Hall, which seated about five thousand people. But the crowds were so great that some days we had to divide the crowds and have women only in the afternoon, and men only at night. One Sunday afternoon the Sydney Town Hall was packed with women. When I gave out the invitation for all who would accept Jesus Christ as their personal Saviour, and surrender to Him as their Lord and Master, and begin to confess Him as such before the world, and so strive to live from this time on as to please Him in every way from day to day, over on my left a whole row of young women of, I should say, about twenty years of age, rose to their feet, eighteen in all. As I saw them stand side by side, I said to myself, "That is someone's Bible class." Afterward they came down forward with the other women who came to make a public confession of their acceptance of Jesus Christ. When the meeting was over, a young lady came to me, her face wreathed in smiles, and said, "That is my Bible class; I have been praying for their conversion, and every one of them has accepted Jesus Christ today."

When we were holding meetings in Bristol, England, a

prominent manufacturer in Exeter had a Bible class of twenty-two men in that city. He invited all of them to go to Bristol with him and hear me preach. Twenty-one of them consented to go. At that meeting twenty of them accepted Christ. The twenty-first accepted Christ in the train on the way home, and then they all, on their return, gathered around the remaining one who would not go, and he also accepted Christ. That manufacturer was praying for the conversion of the members of his class and was willing to make the sacrifices necessary to get his prayers answered. What a revival we would have here in this city if all the Sunday-school teachers would go to praying the way they ought for the conversion of every pupil in his or her class!

Are you in more public work, a preacher perhaps, or speaking from the public platform? Do you long for power in that work? Ask for it. I shall never forget a scene I witnessed many years ago in Boston. It was at the International Christian Workers' Convention, held in the old Tremont Temple, seating thirty-five hundred people. It was my privilege to preside at the convention. On a Saturday morning at eleven o'clock the Tremont Temple was packed to its utmost capacity; every seat was taken, every inch of standing room where men and women were allowed to stand was taken, and multitudes outside were still clamoring for admission. The audience was as fine in its quality as it was large in its numbers. As I looked back of me on the platform, it seemed as if every leading minister and clergyman, not only of Boston, but of New England, was on that platform. Looking down in front of me, I saw seated there the leaders, not only in the church life, but in the social and commercial and political life of Boston and the surrounding country.

I rose to announce the next speaker on the program, and my heart sank, for the next speaker was a woman. In those days I had a prejudice against any woman speaking in public under any circumstances. But this particular woman was a professing Christian, and a Presbyterian at that (and I suppose that is orthodox enough for most of us), but she had been what we call a "worldly Christian," a dancing, card-playing, theater-going, low-necked-dress Christian. She had had, however, an experience of which I had not heard. One night, sitting in their beautiful home in New York City, for she was a woman of wealth, she turned to her husband as he sat reading the evening paper, and said: "Husband, I hear they are doing a good work down at Jerry McAuley's Mission at 316 Water Street. Let us go down and help them." He was a man of very much the same type as she was a woman, kind-hearted, generous, but very much of a worldling. He laid aside his paper and said: "Well, let us go." They put on their wraps and started for 316 Water Street.

When they got there they found the Mission Hall very full and took seats down by the door. As they sat there and listened to one after another of those rescued men, they were filled with new interest, a new world seemed opening to them; and, at last, the woman turned to her husband and whispered: "I guess they will have to help us instead of our helping them. They've got something we haven't." And when the invitation was given out this finely dressed, cultured gentleman and his wife went forward and knelt down at the altar in the sawdust along with the drunken "bums" and other outcasts of Water Street, and they got real salvation.

But of this I knew nothing. I knew only the type of woman she had been, and when I saw her name on the program, as I said, my heart sank and I thought, "What a waste of a magnificent opportunity: here is this wonderful audience and only this woman to speak to them." But I had no authority to change the program; my business was simply to announce it. And summoning all the courtesy I could command under the circumstances, I introduced this lady, and then sank into the chairman's seat and buried my face in my hands and began to pray to God to save us from disaster. Some years afterward I was in Atlanta, and one of the leading Christian workers of that city, who had been at the Boston Convention, came to me, laughing, and said: "I shall never forget how you introduced Mrs. —— at the Boston Convention, and then dropped into your chair and covered your face with your hands as if you had done something you were ashamed of."

Well, I had. But as I said, I began to pray. In a little while I took my face out of my hands and began to watch as well as pray. Every one of those thirty-five hundred pairs of eyes were riveted on that little woman as she stood there and spoke. Soon I saw tears come into eyes that were unaccustomed to weeping, and I saw men and women taking out their handkerchiefs and at first trying to pretend they were not weeping, and then, throwing all disguise to the winds, I saw them bow their heads on the backs of the seats in front of them and sob as if their hearts would break. And before that wonderful address was over that whole audience was swept by the power of that woman's words as the trees of our Western forests sometimes are swept by the cyclone.

This was Saturday morning. The following Monday morning Dr. Broadbeck, at that time pastor of the leading Methodist church in Boston, came to me and said with a choking voice, "Brother Torrey, I could not open my mouth to speak to my own people in my own church yesterday morning without bursting into tears as I thought of that wonderful scene we witnessed here on Saturday morning." When that wonderful address was over, some of us went to this woman and said to her: "God has wonderfully used you this morning." "Oh," she replied, "would you like to know the secret of it? Last night as I thought of the great throng that would fill the Tremont Temple this morning, and of my own inexperience in public address, I spent the whole night on my face before God in prayer." Oh, men and women, if we would spend more nights before God on our faces in prayer there would be more days of power when we faced our congregations!

V. The Prayer of Faith

*And this is the confidence that we have in him, that, if
we ask anything according to his will, he heareth us: and if
we know that he heareth us, whatsoever we ask, we know
that we have the petitions that we have asked of him.*

1 JOHN 5:14, 15 (cf. R.V.).

PLEASE NOTICE carefully exactly what God tells us in this
passage. Here we are told that there is a way in which cer-
tain people can pray so as not only to get the very thing
that they ask, but also as to know before they actually get
it, that God has heard their prayer and that therefore the
thing which they have asked of Him He has granted to
them. Listen again to these wonderful words that the Holy
Spirit inspired John to write: "This is the confidence that
we have in him [that is, in God], that, if we ask anything
according to his will, he heareth us: and if we know that
he heareth us, whatsoever we ask, we know that we have
the petitions that we desired [more literally, have asked]
of him." Certainly that is an astonishing statement: it gives
us the plain and positive assurance that there are some peo-
ple who can pray in a certain way, and that if those people
pray in that way they will not only get whatsoever they
ask, but that, furthermore, they may know before they get
it that God has heard their prayer and granted what they
have asked. It is certainly a great joy when one prays to

58

be able to know that the prayer we have offered has been heard and that what we have asked has been granted, and to be just as sure that it is ours as we shall be when we actually have it in our hand.

I. To Whom the Promise Is Made

Please note, first of all, just who it is to whom God makes this promise. As I have said so often before, when you try to understand and apply the promises of God which you find in the Bible you must always be very careful to note just exactly who the people are to whom the promise is made. Just who the persons are to whom this promise is made we are told in the immediate context, in the verse that immediately precedes, "These things have I written unto you, that ye may know that ye have eternal life, even unto you that believe on the name of the Son of God." Then immediately follows the promise that we are studying today, so it is as clear as day that the promise is made to those who "believe on the name of the Son of God," to them and to nobody else, and anyone who does not believe on the name of the Son of God has no right whatever to take this promise to himself, or to think that if he does take the promise to himself and it is not fulfilled, God's Word has failed. The fault is with himself, and not with God's Word. He has taken to himself a promise that was made to somebody else. Just what it means to believe on the Son of God we are told in the Gospel written by the same one who wrote this Epistle, the Gospel of John; John 1:12: "But as many as received him [that is, received Jesus Christ], to them gave he the right to become children of God, even to them that believe on his name."

So John himself interprets "believing on the name of the Son of God" to mean receiving the Son of God, that is, receiving Him to be to ourselves what He offers Himself to be to all who put their trust in Him, our personal Saviour, who bore our sins in His own body on the cross, and our Lord and Master to whom we surrender the absolute control of our thoughts, our will, and our conduct. So, then, this promise is made to those who have received Jesus Christ as their personal Saviour and trusted God to forgive them because Jesus Christ died on the cross in their place, and also who have received Him as their Lord and Master to whom they have surrendered the absolute control of their thoughts, their will, and their conduct, those who have made an absolute surrender to Jesus Christ, the Son of God. It is made to them, and to no one else, and no one else has the least right to claim it.

Just here is where many go astray, they do not really "believe on the name of the Son of God," they have not really "received him," yet they appropriate to themselves this promise that was never made to them.

II. How We Must Pray in Order to Know that God Has Heard Our Prayers and Granted the Thing that We Have Asked

Now we come to the question, How must "those who believe on the name of the Son of God" pray in order to know that God has heard their prayer, and has granted the thing that they asked? Read the fourteenth verse again. "And this is the confidence that we have in him, that, if we ask anything according to his will, he heareth us." In order to know that God has heard our prayer and granted us what we asked, we must pray according to His will. When we who believe on the name of the Son of God pray for anything that we know to be according to His will, then we may know, for the all-sufficient reason that God says so in His Word, that God has heard the prayer and granted us what we asked. We may know it, not because we feel it, not because of any inward illumination of the Holy Spirit; we may know it for the very best of all reasons—because God says so in His Word, and "God cannot lie."

But is it possible for us to know what the will of God is, so that we can be sure while we are praying that we are asking something that is "according to his will"? We can know the will of God with absolute certainty in many cases when we pray. *How can we know the will of God?*

1. In the first place, we may know the will of God by the promises in His Word. The Bible was given us for the specific purpose of revealing to us the will of God, and when we find that anything is definitely promised in the Word of God we know that that is His will, for He has said so in so many words. And when we who believe on the name of the Son of God go to God and ask Him for anything that is definitely promised in His Word, we may know with absolute certainty that God has heard our prayer and that what we have asked of God is granted. We do not have to feel it—God says so, and that is enough.

For example, God says in His Word, James 1:5, R.V., "If any of you lacketh wisdom, let him ask of God, who giveth to all liberally and upbraideth not; and it shall be given him." So when I go to God and ask for wisdom, if I am a believer on the name of the Son of God, I know with absolute certainty that God has heard my prayer and that wisdom will be granted.

Some years ago I was speaking at a Y.M.C.A. Bible Conference at Mahtomede, White Bear Lake, Minnesota; I was speaking on the subject of prayer. I had to hurry immediately from the amphitheater to the train. As I passed out of the amphitheater I saw another minister from Minneapolis, who was to follow me immediately on the program. He was greatly excited. He stopped me and said, "Mr. Torrey, I am going to tear to pieces everything that you have said to these young men this morning." I replied, "If I have not spoken according to the Bible, I hope you will tear it to pieces. But if I have spoken according to the Book you had better be careful how you try to tear it to pieces." "But," he exclaimed, "you have produced upon these young men the impression that they can pray for things and get the very thing that they ask for." I replied, "I do not know whether that is the impression that I have produced or not, but it certainly is the impression that I intended to produce."

"But," he said, "that is not right; you must say if it be according to God's will." I replied, "If you do not know that the thing which you have asked is according to God's will, then it is all right to say, 'If it be according to Thy will.' But if you know God's will, what is the need of saying, 'If it be according to Thy will'?" "But," he said, "we cannot know God's will." I answered, "What was the Bible given to us for if it was not to reveal God's will? Now," I said, "when you find a definite promise in the Bible and take that promise to God, don't you know that you have asked something according to His will? For example, we read in James 1:5, 'If any of you lacketh wisdom, let him ask of God, who giveth to all liberally and upbraideth not; and it shall be given him.' Now," I said, "when you ask for wisdom do you not know that God is going to give it?" "But," he said, "I do not know what wisdom is." I said, "If you did you would not need to ask it, but whatever it may be, do you not know that God is going to give it?" He made no reply. I never heard that he tried to tear what I said to pieces, but I know that later he himself spoke very boldly on the subject of confidently asking God for the things that we need of Him, and that are according to His will.

No, when you have a definite promise in God's Word you do not need to put any "ifs" before it. All the promises of God are yea and amen in Christ Jesus (II Cor. 1:20). They are absolutely sure, and if you plead any plain promise in God's Word you need not put any "ifs" in your petition. You may know that you are asking something that is according to God's will, and it is your privilege to know that God has heard you, and it is your privilege to know that you have the thing you have asked; it is your privilege to get up from prayer with the same absolute certainty that that thing is yours that you will afterward have when you actually see it in your hand.

Suppose some cold winter morning when I lived in Chicago I had gone down on South Clark Street that was then teeming with poor men, and some shivering tramp should have come up to me and said, "Mr. Torrey, it is very cold and I need an overcoat. Will you give me an overcoat?" And then I had replied, "If you will come over to my house this afternoon at 39 East Pearson Street, at two o'clock, I'll give you an overcoat." Promptly at two o'clock the tramp makes his appearance. I meet him at the door and bring him into the house. Then he says to me, "Mr. Torrey, you said to me this morning on South Clark Street that if I would come to your home at two o'clock this afternoon you would give me an overcoat. Now, if you will, please give me that overcoat." What would I say? I'd say, "Man, what did you say?" He would reply, "I said, if you will, please give me that overcoat." "But why do you put any 'if' in? Did I not say I would?" "Yes." "Do you doubt my word?" "No." "Then why do you put in an 'if'?" So why should we put any "ifs" in when we take to God any promise of His own? Does God ever lie? There are many cases in which we do not know the will of God, and in such cases it is all right to put in "if it be Thy will." And even in cases where we do not know His will, our prayers should always be in submission to His will, for the dearest of anything to the true child of God is God's will, but there is no need to put any "ifs" in when He has revealed His will. To put in an "if" in such a case as that is to doubt God, to doubt His Word, and really is to "make God a liar."

This passage of Scripture is one of the most abused passages in the Bible. God put it into His Word to give us "confidence" when we pray. It is constantly misused to make us uncertain when we pray. Oftentimes when some young and enthusiastic believer is asking for something with great confidence, some cautious brother will go to him after the meeting is over and say to him, "Now, my young brother, you must not be so confident as that in your prayers. It may not be God's will, and we ought to be submissive to the will of God, and you should say, 'If it be Thy will.'" And so some men always have an element of uncertainty in their prayers, and one would think that I John 5:14 read, "This is the uncertainty that we have in him, that we can never know God's will, and therefore can never be sure that our prayer is heard." But that is not the way the verse reads. It reads, "This is the confidence [not uncertainty, but absolute confidence] that we have in him, that, if we ask anything according to his will, *he heareth us:* and if we know that he hear us, whatsoever we ask, *we know that we have* the petitions that we have asked of him." Oh, how subtle the devil is to take a passage of

Scripture that God has put into His Word to fill us with confidence when we pray, and use it to make us uncertain when we pray.

2. But can we know the will of God when we pray, even when there is no definite promise in regard to the matter about which we are praying? Yes, in many cases we can. How? Romans 8:26, 27, R.V., answers the question: "And in like manner the Spirit also helpeth our infirmity: for we know not how to pray as we ought; but the Spirit himself maketh intercession for us with groanings which cannot be uttered; and he that searcheth the hearts knoweth what is the mind of the Spirit, because he maketh intercession for the saints according to the will of God." It is the work of the Holy Spirit when we pray to make known to us what is the will of God in the matter about which we are praying, and to show us if the thing is according to His will, that it is according to His will. There are many things we need which are not definitely promised in the Word, and it doesn't follow at all that because they are not definitely promised in the Word they are not "according to the will of God." It is the will of God to give us very many things which He has not definitely promised in His Word, and it is the method of God, when we pray, to give us, by the direct illumination of the Holy Spirit, to know His will even in regard to things about which He has given us no definite promise.

For example, while I was pastor of the Moody Church in Chicago, the child of a man and woman who were both members of our church was taken very sick. The child first had the measles, and the measles was followed by meningitis. The child sank very low, and the doctor said to the mother, "I can do no more for your child. Your child cannot live." She immediately hurried to my house to get me to come up to their house and pray for her child. But I was out of town holding meetings in Pittsburgh. So she sent for my assistant pastor, Rev. W. S. Jacoby, and he went to the house with one of my colleagues in the Bible Institute, and prayed for the child. That night when I got home from Pittsburgh he came around to my house to tell me about it, and he said, "Mr. Torrey, if I ever had an answer to my prayers in my life, it was today when I was praying for the Duff child." He was confident that God had heard his prayer and that the child would be healed. And the child was healed right away. This was Saturday. The next morning the doctor called again at the house and there was such a remarkable change in the child that he said to Mrs. Duff, "What have you done for your child?" She told him just what she had done. Then he said, "Well, I will give her some more medicine." "No," she said, "you will not. You said you could do no more for the child, that the child must die, and we went to God in prayer and God has healed the child. You are not going to take the honor to yourself by giving him some more medicine." Indeed, the child was not only improved that morning, the child was well, and Mrs. Duff was at the morning service and would have brought the child with her if it had not been such a stormy morning that she thought it would be better not to take it out in the intense cold.

Now, neither Mr. Jacoby nor I could pray for every sick child in that way, for it is not the will of God to heal every sick child, nor every sick adult. It is God's general will in regard to His children that they be well in body, but there are cases when God, for wise purposes of His own, does not see fit to heal the sick; and there are cases, if we are living near to God and listening for the voice of His Spirit, and are entirely surrendered to the Spirit in our praying, in which the Spirit of God will make clear to us the will of God, and we shall know that our prayer is heard, and we will know that the request is ours long before we actually get it.

Take another and entirely different illustration, for the healing of the body is only one of the ways in which God answers prayer, and not by any means the most important. In my first pastorate we had a union meeting of all the churches of the town. In the course of the meetings we had a day of fasting and prayer. During the morning meeting while we were praying, God led me to pray that one of the most unlikely men in the town might be saved that night. The man had led a wild, roaming life; few in his family were Christians; but as we knelt in prayer that morning God put a great burden on my heart for that man's salvation, and I prayed that he might come to the meeting and be saved that night. And as I prayed, God gave me great confidence that the man would come and be saved. And come he did, and saved he was, that night. There was not a man in that whole town who was more unlikely to be saved than he. That was more than forty years ago, but when I was in Chattanooga, Tennessee, a few years ago, I met another man whose mother was saved about the same time, and he told me that this man was then living in Tennessee and was still living a Christian life. Now, I cannot pray for the salvation of every unsaved person in that way, but by His Spirit God revealed to me His will regarding that man, and in many a case He has revealed His will.

Take still another illustration. One day, when I was in Northfield, Mass., I received word from Mr. Fitt, Mr. Moody's son-in-law, in Chicago, that we needed five thousand dollars for the work in Chicago at once, and asking me to pray for it. Another member of the faculty of the Bible Institute was in Northfield at that time, and that night we went out into a summer-house on my place and knelt down and prayed God to send that five thousand dollars. And God gave my friend great confidence that He had heard the prayer, and he said to me, "God has heard the prayer and the five thousand dollars will come." Mr. Fitt and Mr. Gaylord also prayed in Chicago, and God gave Mr. Gaylord a great confidence that the five thousand dollars would come. We knew it was ours, we knew that God had heard the prayer and that we had received the five thousand dollars. And a telegram came the next day (I think it was) from Indianapolis, saying that five thousand dollars had been deposited in a bank in Indianapolis to our account and was awaiting our order. Though we had prayed for the money and expected it, Mr. Fitt could hardly believe the news, and sent to our bank in Chicago, which inquired of the bank in Indianapolis if the information were true, and learned that it was. So far as I know, the man who put that money in the bank in Indianapolis at our call had never given a penny to the Bible Institute before. I did not know there was such a man in the world, and, so far as I know, he has never given a penny to the Bible Institute since. Now, I cannot go to God every time I want money and think I need it and ask God for it with that same confidence, but there are times when I can. There have been many such times in my life, and God has never failed, and He never will. Banks sometimes fail; God never fails.

To sum it all up, when God makes known His will, either by a specific promise of His Word or by His Holy Spirit while we are praying, that what we ask for is "according to his will," it is our privilege to know—if we really believe on the name of the Son of God—that our prayer is granted, and that it is ours, just as truly ours, as it will be when later we actually have it in our hand.

III. Praying in Faith

The passage we have been studying is closely related to another passage in the Gospel of Mark, which contains a promise of our Lord Himself that God will answer prayer. It is a very familiar passage; you will find it in Mark 11:24: "Therefore I say unto you, What things soever ye desire, when ye pray, believe that ye receive them, and ye shall have them." I will not stop to call your attention to whom this promise is made, further than to say that it is made, as are all the other promises of God to answer prayer which we have been studying, to those who believe on Jesus Christ, those who are united to Jesus Christ by a living faith that manifests itself in an obedient love. This is evident from the context, as you can find out for yourself if you will read the promise in its context.

And how must we pray in order to get the thing that we ask? We *must pray in faith*, that is, we must pray with confident expectation of getting the very thing that we ask. Some say that any prayer that is in submission to the will of God, and in faith and dependence on Him, is a prayer of faith. But it is not "the prayer of faith" in the Bible sense of "the prayer of faith." "The prayer of faith," in the Bible sense, is the prayer that has no doubt whatever that God has heard and granted the specific thing "which we have asked of him." This is evident from James 1:5-7 R.V.: "But if any of you lacketh wisdom, let him ask of God, who giveth to all liberally and upbraideth not; and it shall be given him. But let him ask in faith, nothing doubting: for he that doubteth is like the surge of the sea driven by the wind and tossed. For let not that man think that he shall receive anything of the Lord." No matter how positive the promises of God may be, he will never receive them in our own experience till we absolutely believe them, and the prayer that gets what it asks is "the prayer of faith," that is, the prayer that has no doubt whatever of getting the very thing that is asked.

This comes out more clearly in the Revised Version of Mark 11:24 than in the Authorized. Let me read you from the English Revision, which is more accurate in this case than the American Revision: "Therefore I say unto you, all things whatsoever ye pray and ask for, believe that ye have received them, and ye shall have them." When we pray to God, and pray according to His will as known by the promises of His Word, or as known by the Holy Spirit revealing His will to us, we should confidently believe that the very thing that we have asked is granted us. We should "believe that" we "have received," and what we thus believe we have received we shall afterward have in actual personal experience.

Take, for example, the matter of praying for "the baptism with the Holy Spirit." When anyone prays for the Holy Spirit, anyone who is united to Jesus Christ by a living faith that reveals itself in an obedient love, anyone who has received Jesus Christ as his Saviour and is trusting God to forgive him on the sole ground that Jesus Christ died in his place, and who has received Jesus Christ as his Lord and Master, and has surrendered all his thoughts and purposes and conduct to God's control, he may know that he has prayed for something according to God's will, for Jesus Christ definitely says in Luke 11:13, "If ye then, being evil, know how to give good gifts unto your children; how much more shall your heavenly Father give the Holy

Spirit to them that ask him?" And as one knows that he has asked something which is according to God's will as God has clearly revealed it in His Word, it is one's privilege to say, "I have what I asked. I have the Holy Spirit." It is not a question at all of whether one feels that he has received the Holy Spirit or not; it is not a question of some remarkable experience: it is simply a question of taking God at His Word and that he who prays believes that he has received, just because God says so. And what he has taken by naked faith on the Word of God, simply believing he has received, because God says so, he will afterward actually possess. There is no need that he go to any "tarrying meeting," no need that he work himself up into a frenzy of emotionalism, no need that he fall into a trance, or fall into unconsciousness, an experience utterly foreign to anything described in the New Testament. He has far better ground for his assurance that he has received what he asked than any feeling or any ecstasy; he has the immutable Word of God, "God who cannot lie."

Praying in faith, that is praying with an unquestioning belief that you will receive just exactly what you ask; yes, believing as you pray that God has heard your prayer and that you have received the thing that you ask, is one of the most important factors in obtaining what we ask when we pray. As James puts it in 1:6, 7, "Let him ask in faith, nothing doubting: for he that doubteth is like the surge of the sea driven by the wind and tossed. For let not that man think that he shall receive anything of the Lord." That is, let not the man who has any doubt that God has heard his prayer think that he shall receive anything of the Lord.

So the tremendously important question arises, How can we pray the prayer of faith? How can we pray with a confident, unquestioning certainty in our minds that God has heard our prayer and granted the thing that we ask? This has been partly answered in what we have already said, but in order that it may be perfectly clear, let us repeat the substance of it again.

1. To pray the prayer of faith we must, first of all, study the Word of God, especially the promises of God, and find out what the will of God is and build our prayers on the written promises of God. Intelligent faith, and that is the only kind of faith that counts with God, must have a warrant. We cannot believe by just trying to make ourselves believe. Such belief as that is not faith but credulity, it is "make-believe."

The great warrant for intelligent faith is God's Word. As Paul puts it in Romans 10:17, "Faith cometh by hearing, and hearing by the word of God." The faith that is built on the sure Word of God is an intelligent faith, it has something to rest on. So if we would pray the prayer of faith we must study much the Word of God and find out what God has definitely promised, and then, with God's promise in mind, approach God and ask Him for that thing which He has promised.

Here is the point at which many go astray. Here is the point at which I went astray in my early prayer life. Not long after my conversion I got hold of this promise of our Lord Jesus in Mark 11:24, "Therefore I say unto you. What things soever ye desire, when ye pray, believe that ye receive them, and ye shall have them." I said to myself, "All that I need to do if I want anything is to ask God for it and then make myself believe that I am going to get it, and I'll have it." So whenever I wanted anything I asked God for it and tried to make myself believe I was going to get it, but I didn't get it, for it was only "make-believe" and I did not really believe at all. But I later learned that "faith cometh by hearing, and hearing by the Word of God," and that if I wished to pray "the prayer of faith" I must have some warrant for my faith, some ground on which to rest my faith, and that the surest of all grounds for faith was the Word of God. So when I desired anything of God I would search the Scriptures to find if there was some promise that covered that case, and then go to God and plead His own promise; and thus resting on that promise I would believe that God had heard, and He had, and I got what I asked.

One of the mightiest men of prayer of the last generation was George Mueller of Bristol, England, who in the last sixty years of his life (he lived to be ninety-two or ninety-three) obtained the English equivalent of seven million four hundred dollars by prayer. But George Mueller never prayed for something just because he wanted it, or even just because he felt it was greatly needed for God's work. When it was laid on George Mueller's heart to pray for anything, he would search the Scriptures to find if there was some promise that covered the case. Sometimes he would search the Scriptures for days before he presented his petition to God. And then, when he found the promise, with his open Bible before him and his finger on that promise, he would plead that promise and so he received what he asked. He always prayed with an open Bible before him.

2. But this is not all that is to be said about how to pray "the prayer of faith." It is possible for us to have faith in many an instance when there is no definite promise covering the case, and to pray with the absolute assurance that God has heard our prayer, to believe with a faith that has not a shadow of doubt in it that we have received what we have asked. The way that comes to pass we are plainly told

in the passage to which I have already referred in the earlier part of this sermon, Romans 8:26, 27, R.V.: "In like manner the Spirit also helpeth our infirmity: for we know not how to pray as we ought; but the Spirit himself maketh intercession for us with groanings which cannot be uttered, and he that searcheth the hearts knoweth what is the mind of the Spirit, because he maketh intercession for the saints according to the will of God." That is to say, the Holy Spirit, as we have already said, oftentimes makes clear to us as we pray what it is the will of God to do, so that, listening to His voice, we can pray with absolute confidence, with a confidence that has not a shadow of doubt, that God has heard our prayer and granted the thing that was asked.

My first experience, at least the first that I recall, of this wonderful privilege of knowing the will of God, and praying with confident faith even when one had no definite promise in the written Word that God would hear the prayer, came very early in my ministry. There was a young dentist in my congregation whose father was a member of our church. This dentist was taken very ill with typhoid fever, and went down to the very gates of death. I went to see him and found him unconscious. The doctor and his father were by the bedside, and the doctor said to me, "He cannot live. The crisis is past and it has turned the wrong way. There is no possibility of his recovery." I knelt down to pray, and as I prayed a great confidence came into my heart, an absolutely unshakable confidence that God had heard my prayer and that the man was to be raised up. As I rose from my knees I said to the father and the doctor, "Ebbie will get well. He will not die at this time." The doctor smiled and said, "That is all right, Mr. Torrey, from your standpoint, but he cannot live. He will die." I replied, "Doctor, that is all right from your standpoint, but he cannot die; he will live." I went home. Not long after, word was brought to me that the young man was dying. They told me what he was doing, and said that no one ever did that except just when he was dying. I calmly replied, "He is not dying. He will not die. He will get well." I knew he would: he did. The last I knew of him he was still living, and his healing took place between forty and forty-five years ago. But I cannot pray for every sick man in that way, not even though he is an earnest Christian, as this man was not at that time. Sometimes it is God's will to heal, usually it is God's will to heal, if the conditions are met; but it is not always God's will to heal. "The prayer of faith shall save the sick," God tells us in James 5:15; but it is not always possible to pray "the prayer of faith"; we can pray it only when God makes it possible by the leading of His Holy Spirit.

But "the prayer of faith" will not only heal the sick, it will bring many other blessings, blessings of far more importance than physical healing. It will bring salvation to the lost; it will bring power into our service; it will bring money into the treasury of the Lord; it will bring great revivals of religion. In my first pastorate one of the first persons to accept Christ was a woman who had been a backslider for many years. But she not only came back to the Lord, but came back in a very thorough way. Not long after her conversion God gave to her a great spirit of prayer for a revival in our church and community. When I had been there about a year she was called to go out to California with a sick friend, but before going she came into the prayer meeting on her last prayer-meeting night there, and said, "God has heard my prayer for a revival. You are going to have a great revival here in the church."

And we did have a revival, not only in the church, but in the whole community, a revival that transformed every church in the community and brought many souls to Christ. And the revival went on again the next year, and the next, and the next, until I left that field. And it went on under the pastor who followed me and the pastor who followed him.

Oh, yes, "the prayer of faith" is the great secret of getting the things of all kinds that we need in our personal life, that we need in our service, that we need in our work, that we need in our church, that we need everywhere. There is no limit to what "the prayer of faith can do," and if we would pray more and pray more intelligently, and pray "the prayer of faith," there is no telling what we could do as a church and as an institute.* But as we have said, in order to pray "the prayer of faith" we must, first of all, study our Bible much in order that we may know the promises of God, what they are, how large they are, how definite they are, and just exactly what is promised. In addition to that, we must live so near to God, be so fully surrendered to the will of God, have such a delight in God and so feel our utter dependence on the Spirit of God, that the Holy Spirit Himself can guide us in our prayers and indicate clearly to us what the will of God is, and make us sure while we pray that we have asked for something that is according to God's will, and thus enable us to pray with the absolute confidence that God has heard our prayer, and that "we have received" the things that we asked of Him.

Here is where many of us fail in our prayer life: We either do not know that it is our privilege to "pray in the Spirit," that is, to pray under the Spirit's guidance; or else

* Moody Bible Institute.

we do not realize our utter dependence on the Holy Spirit, and cast ourselves on Him to lead us when we pray, and therefore we pray for the things which our own heart, our own selfish desire, prompts us to pray for; or else we are not in such an attitude toward God that the Spirit of God can make His voice heard in our hearts.

Oh that we might all be made to realize the immeasurable blessings for ourselves, for our friends, and for the church and for the world, that lie within the reach of "the prayer of faith," and determine that we would pray "the prayer of faith"; and then get down to the study of the Word of God so that we could know God's will and what to pray for; and be in such a relation toward God, be so fully surrendered to His will and in utter, constant dependence on the Holy Spirit, looking to the Holy Spirit that as we pray it might not be so much we who pray as the Holy Spirit praying through us! Then we would soon see this spiritual-desert city of ———, and our spiritual-desert churches, "blossom as the rose."

VI. How to Pray

*But prayer was made earnestly of the church unto God
for him.*

ACTS 12:5, R.V.

OUR SUBJECT is, "How to Pray So As to Get What You
Ask." I can think of nothing more important that I could
tell you. Suppose it had been announced that I was to tell
the business men of this city how they could go to any
bank here and get all the financial accommodation they de-
sired any day in the year, and suppose, also, that I knew
that secret and could really tell it, do you think that the
business men of this city would consider the information
important? It would be difficult to think of anything that
they would consider more important. But praying is going
to the bank, going to the bank that has the largest capital
of any bank in the universe, the Bank of Heaven, a bank
whose capital is absolutely unlimited. And if I can show
you this morning how you can go to the Bank of Heaven
any day in the year, and any hour of the day or night, and
get from that bank all that you desire, that will certainly
be of incalculable importance.

Now, the Bible tells us that very thing. It tells us how
we can go to the Bank of Heaven, how we can go to God
in prayer any day of the year and any hour of the day or
night, and get from God the very things that we ask. What

the Bible teaches along this line has been put to the test of practical experiment by tens of thousands of people, and has been found in their own experience to be absolutely true. And that is what we are to discover from a study of God's own Word.

In the twelfth chapter of the Acts of the Apostles we have the record of a most remarkable prayer, remarkable because of what was asked for and remarkable because of the results of the asking. King Herod had killed James, the brother of John. This greatly "pleased the Jews," so he proceeded further to arrest the leader of the whole apostolic company, the Apostle Peter, with the intention of killing him also. But the arrest was during Passover Week, the Holy Week of the Jews; and, while the Jews were perfectly willing to have Peter assassinated, eager to have him assassinated, they were not willing to have their Holy Week desecrated by his violent death. So Peter was cast into prison to be kept until the Passover week was over, and then to be executed. The Passover week was nearly over, it was the last night of the Passover week, and early the next morning Peter was to be taken out and beheaded.

There seemed to be little hope for Peter, indeed, no hope at all. He was in a secure dungeon, in an impregnable fortress, guarded by sixteen soldiers, and chained by each wrist to a soldier who slept on either side of him. There appeared to be no hope whatever for Peter. But the Christians in Jerusalem undertook to get Peter out of his perilous position, to completely deliver him. How did they go at it? Did they organize a mob and storm the castle? No, there was no hope whatever of success that way. The castle was impregnable against any mob, and, furthermore, it was garrisoned by trained Roman soldiers who would be more than a match for any mob. Did the Christians circulate a petition and get the names of the leading Christians in Jerusalem signed to it to present to Herod, asking that he would release Peter? No. That might have had weight, for the Christians in Jerusalem at that time were numbered by the thousands and among them were not a few influential persons, and a petition signed by so many people, and by some people of such weight, would have had influence with a wily politician such as Herod was. But the Christians did not attempt that method of deliverance. Did they take up a collection and gather a large amount of money from the believers in Jerusalem to bribe Herod to release Peter? Quite likely that might have proved successful, for Herod was open to that method of approach. But they did not do that.

What did they do? They held a prayer meeting to pray Peter out of prison. Was anything apparently more futile and ridiculous ever undertaken by a company of fanatics? Praying a man so securely incarcerated, and so near his execution, out of prison? If the enemies of Peter and the church had known of that attempt they doubtless would have been greatly amused, and have laughed at the thought of these fanatical Christians praying Peter out of prison, and doubtless would have said to one another, "We'll see what will become of the prayers of these fool Christians."

But the attempt to pray Peter out of prison was entirely successful. Apparently Peter himself had no fears, but was calmly resting in God; for he was fast asleep on the very eve of his proposed execution. While Peter was sound asleep, guarded by the sixteen soldiers, chained to a soldier sleeping on either side of him, suddenly there shone in the prison a light, a light from heaven; and "an angel of God" could have been seen standing by Peter. The angel "smote Peter on the side" as he slept, and wakened him, and said, "Arise up quickly." Instantly Peter's chains fell from his hands and he arose to his feet. The angel said to him, "Gird thyself, and bind on thy sandals." Peter did so, and then the angel said, "Cast thy garment about thee, and follow me." Peter, dazed and wondering, thought he was dreaming; but he was wise enough to obey God even in his sleep and he went out and followed the angel, though he "thought he saw a vision." The soldiers were all asleep, and, unhindered, the angel and Peter passed the first guard and the second guard and came to the strong iron gate that led into the city. Moved by the finger of God, the gate "opened to them of its own accord." They went out and silently passed through one street.

Now Peter was safe, and the angel left him. Standing there in the cold night air, Peter came to himself, and realized that he was not dreaming, and said, "Now I know of a truth, that the Lord has sent forth his angel to deliver me out of the hand of Herod, and from all the expectation of the people of the Jews." Stopping a few moments to reflect, he said to himself, "There is a prayer meeting going on. It must be at Mark's mother's house; I will go there." And soon the pray-ers are startled by a heavy pounding at the outside gate of Mark's mother's home. A little servant girl named Rhoda was kneeling among the pray-ers. Instantly she sprang to her feet and rushed to the gate, saying to herself, "That's Peter! That's Peter! I knew God would hear our prayers. God has delivered him, and he is at the gate." Reaching the gate, she excitedly cried, "Is that you, Peter?" "Yes." Forgetting even to open the gate, and leaving Peter standing outside, she dashed back and said to the startled pray-ers, "Our prayers are answered—

Peter is at the gate." "Oh, Rhoda, you are crazy," cried the unbelieving company. "No," Rhoda said, "I am not crazy. It is Peter. God has answered our prayers. I know his voice. I knew he would come and he is here." Then they all cried, "It is not Peter, it is his ghost. He has been killed in the night and his ghost has come around and is rapping at the gate." But Peter kept on knocking, and they opened the gate, and there stood Peter, the living evidence that God has answered their prayer.

By the way, have you ever noticed that among all the company that were present at that prayer meeting only one person is mentioned by name, and that one person only a servant girl, Rhoda? Doubtless the bishops and elders of the Church in Jerusalem were there, but not a single name of theirs has come down to us. Probably some of the leading people of Jerusalem who had now become Christians were there, but not a single name is mentioned. Rhoda, and Rhoda only. Why? Because Rhoda was the only one who really had faith and was therefore the only one worth mentioning, even though she was only a servant girl. "Rhoda" means rose, and this Rhoda was a rose very fragrant to God, although she was only a servant girl; for there is no sweeter fragrance to God than the fragrance of faith.

Now, if we can find out how these people prayed, then we shall know just how we, too, can pray so as to get what we ask. In the fifth verse we are told exactly how they prayed. Let me read it to you. "Prayer was made without ceasing of the church unto God for him." The whole secret of prevailing prayer, the prayer that gets what it asks, is found in four phrases in this brief description of their prayer. The first phrase is, "without ceasing." The second, "of the Church." The third, "unto God." The fourth, "for him."

I. Unto God

Let us take up these four phrases and study them. We take up first the third phrase, for it is really the most important one, "unto God." The prayer that gets what it asks is the prayer that is *unto God*. But someone will say, "Is not all prayer unto God?" No. Comparatively few of the prayers that go up from this earth today are really unto God. I sometimes think that not one prayer in a hundred is really "unto God." You ask, "What do you mean?" I mean exactly what I say, that not one prayer in a hundred is really unto God. "Oh," you say, "I know what you mean. You are talking about the prayers of the heathen unto their idols and their false gods." No, I mean the prayers of people who call themselves Christians. I do not think that one in a hundred of them is really unto God. "Oh," you say, "I know what you mean. You are talking of the prayers of the Roman Catholics unto the Virgin Mary and unto the saints." No, I mean the prayers of people who call themselves Protestants. I do not believe that one in a hundred of the prayers of Protestant believers is really unto God. "What do you mean?" you ask. I mean exactly what I say.

Stop a moment and think. Is it not often the case, when men stand up to pray in public, or kneel down to pray in private, that they are thinking far more of what they are asking for than they are of the great God who made heaven and earth, and who has all power? Is it not often the case that in our prayers we are not thinking much of either what we are asking for or of Him from whom we are asking it, but, instead, our thoughts are wandering off wool-gathering everywhere? We take the name of God on our lips, but there is no real conscious approach to God in our hearts. We are really taking the name of God in vain when we fancy we are praying to Him. If there is to be any power in our prayer, if our prayer is to get anything, the first thing to be sure of when we pray is that we really have come into the presence of God, and are really speaking to Him. We should never utter one syllable of prayer, either in public or in private, until we are definitely conscious that we have come into the presence of God and are actually praying to Him. Oh, let those two words, "Unto God," "Unto God," "*Unto God*," sink deep into your heart; and from this time on never pray, never utter one syllable of prayer, until you are sure that you have come into the presence of God and are really talking to Him.

Some years ago in our church in Chicago, before we began the great Saturday night prayer meetings to pray for a world-wide revival, a little group of us used to meet every Saturday night for prayer, to pray for God's blessing on the work of the morrow. Never more than a handful of people came, but we had wonderful times of blessing. One night, after we had gathered together, I rose to open the meeting and said to those gathered there, "Now we are going to kneel in prayer and every one of you feel at perfect liberty to ask for what God puts into your heart to ask for; but be sure that you do not utter a word of prayer until you have really come into the presence of God, and know that you are talking to Him." Then we knelt in prayer. A friend of mine, a business man, had come in just before I said that. One day the following week I met him and he said to me, "Mr. Torrey, I ought to be ashamed to confess it, but do you know that that thought you threw out last Saturday night just before we knelt in prayer, that not one of us should utter a syllable of prayer until we had really come into the presence of

God and knew that we were talking to Him, was an entirely new thought to me and it has transformed my prayer life?" I could easily understand that, for I can remember when that thought transformed my prayer life. I was brought up to pray. I was taught to pray so early in life that I have not the slightest recollection of who taught me to pray. I have no doubt it was my mother, but I have no recollection of it. In my earliest days the habit of prayer was so thoroughly ingrained into me that there has never been a single night of my life as far back as my memory goes, that I have not prayed; with the exception of one night when I was carried home unconscious and did not regain consciousness until the next morning.

Even when I had wandered far from God, and had definitely decided that I would not accept Jesus Christ, I still prayed every night. Even when I had come to a place where I doubted that the Bible was the Word of God, and that Jesus Christ was the Son of God, and even doubted that there was a personal God, nevertheless, I prayed every night. I am glad that I was brought up that way, and that the habit of prayer was so instilled into me that it became permanent, for it was through that habit that I came back out of the darkness of agnosticism into the clear light of an intelligent faith in God and His Word. Nevertheless, prayer was largely a mere matter of form. There was little real thought of God, and no real approach to God. And even after I was converted, yes, even after I had entered the ministry, prayer was largely a matter of form. But the day came when I realized what real prayer meant, realized that prayer was having an audience with God, actually coming into the presence of God and asking and getting things from Him. And the realization of that fact transformed my prayer life. Before that, prayer had been a mere duty, and sometimes a very irksome duty, but from that time on prayer has been not merely a duty but a privilege, one of the most highly esteemed privileges of life. Before that, the thought I had was, "How much time must I spend in prayer?" The thought that now possesses me is, "How much time may I spend in prayer without neglecting the other privileges and duties of life?"

Suppose some Englishman were summoned to Buckingham Palace to meet King George. He answers the summons and is waiting in the anteroom to be ushered into the presence of the King. What do you think that man would say to himself while he waited to be brought into the presence of the King? Do you think he would say, "I wonder how much time I must spend with the King?" No, indeed; he would think, "I wonder how much time the King will give me." But prayer is having an audience with the King of kings, that eternal, omnipotent King, in comparison with whom all earthly kings are as nothing; and would any intelligent person who realizes that fact ever ask himself, "How much time must I spend in prayer?" No, our thought will be, "How much time may I spend in prayer, how much time will the King give me?"

So let these two words, "unto God," sink deep into your heart and govern your prayer life from this day on. Whenever you kneel in prayer, or stand in prayer, whether it be in public or in private, be absolutely sure before you utter a syllable of prayer that you have actually come into the presence of God and are really speaking to Him. Oh, it is a wondrous secret.

But at this point a question arises. How can we come into the presence of God, and how can we be sure that we have come into the presence of God, and that we are really talking to Him? Some years ago I was speaking on this verse of Scripture in Chicago, and at the close of the address a very intelligent Christian woman, one of the most intelligent and deeply spiritual women I ever knew, came to me and said, "Mr. Torrey, I like that thought of 'unto God,' but how can we come into the presence of God and how can we be absolutely sure that we have come into the presence of God, and that we are really talking to Him?" It was a wise question and a question of great importance; and it is clearly answered in the Word of God. There are two parts to the answer.

1. You will find the first part of the answer in the Epistle to the Hebrews, chapter ten, verse nineteen, "Having therefore, brethren, boldness to enter into the holiest by the blood of Jesus." That is the first part of the answer. We come into the presence of God "by the blood of Jesus"; and we can come into the presence of God in no other way. Just what does that mean? It means this: You and I are sinners, the best of us are great sinners, and God is infinitely holy, so holy that even the seraphim, those wonderful "burning ones" (for that is what seraphim means, burning ones), burning in their own intense holiness, must veil their faces and their feet in His presence (Is. 6:2). But our sins have been laid on another; they were laid on the Lord Jesus when He died on the cross of Calvary and made a perfect atonement for our sins. When He died there He took our place, the place of rejection by God, the place of the "curse," and the moment we accept Him and believe God's testimony concerning His blood, that by His shed blood He made perfect atonement for our sin, and trust God to forgive and justify us because the Lord Jesus died in our place, that moment our sins are forgiven and we are reckoned righteous and enter into a place above the seraphim, the place of God's only and perfect

Son, Jesus Christ. And we do not need to veil our faces or our feet when we come into His presence, for we are made perfectly "accepted in the beloved" (Eph. 1:6). To "enter into the holiest," then, to come into the very presence of God, "by the blood of Jesus," means that when we draw near to God we should give up any and every thought that we have any acceptability before God in ourselves, realize that we are miserable sinners, and also believe that every sin of ours has been atoned for by the shed blood of Jesus Christ, and therefore come "with boldness" into the very presence of God, "into the holiest, by the blood of Jesus." The best man or woman on earth cannot come into the presence of God on the ground of any merit of his own, not for one moment; nor get anything from God on the ground of his own goodness, not even the smallest blessing. But on the ground of the shed blood of Jesus Christ the vilest sinner who ever walked this earth, who has turned from his sin and accepted Jesus Christ and trusts in the shed blood as the ground of his acceptance before God, can come into the presence of God any day of the year, and any hour of the day or night, and with perfect boldness speak out every longing of his heart and get what he asks from God. Isn't that wonderful? Yes, and, thank God, it is true.

Christian Scientists cannot really pray. What they call prayer is simply meditation or concentration of thought. It is not asking a personal God for a definite blessing; indeed, Mrs. Eddy denies the existence of a personal God, and she denies the atoning efficacy of the blood. She said that when the blood of Jesus Christ was shed on the cross of Calvary it did no more good than when it was running in His veins. So a Christian Scientist cannot really pray; he is not on praying ground.

Neither can a Unitarian really pray. Oh, he can take the name of God on his lips and call Him Father, and say beautiful words, but there is no real approach to God. Our Lord Jesus Christ Himself said, "I am the way, the truth, and the life: no man cometh unto the Father, but by [more literally, through] me." Some years ago in Chicago I was on a committee of three persons, one of whom was one of the leading Unitarian ministers of the city. He was a charming man in many ways. One day, at the close of our committee meeting, this Unitarian minister turned to me and said, "Brother Torrey, I often come over to your church to hear you." I replied, "I am very glad to hear it." Then he continued, "I especially love to go to your prayer meetings. Often of a Friday night I drop into your prayer meeting and sit down by the door, and I greatly enjoy it." I replied, "I am glad that you do. But tell me something. Why don't you have a prayer meeting in your own church?" "Well," he said, "you have asked me an honest question and I will give you an honest answer. Because I can't. I have tried it and it has failed every time." Of course it failed, they had no ground of approach to God—they denied the atoning blood.

But there is many a supposedly orthodox Christian, and often in these days even supposedly orthodox ministers, who deny the atoning blood. They do not believe that the forgiveness of our sins is solely and entirely on the ground of the shedding of Jesus' blood as an atonement for sin on our behalf on the cross of Calvary, and, therefore, they cannot really pray. There are not a few who call the theology that insists on the truth so very clearly taught in the Word of God, the doctrine of the substitutionary character of Christ's death and that we are saved by the shedding of His blood, a "theology of the shambles" (that is, of the butcher shop).

Mr. Alexander and I were holding meetings in the Royal Albert Hall in London. I received through the mail one day one of our hymnbooks that some man had taken from the meeting. He had gone through it and cut out every reference to the blood of Christ. With the hymnbook was an accompanying letter, in which the man said, "I have gone through your hymnbook and cut out every reference to the blood in every place where it is found, and I am sending this hymnbook back to you. Now sing your hymns this way, with the blood left out, and there will be some sense in them." I took the hymnbook to the meeting with me that afternoon and displayed it; it was a sadly mutilated book. I read the man's letter, and then I said, "No, I will not cut the blood out of my hymnology, and I will not cut the blood out of my theology, for when I cut the blood out of my hymnology and my theology I will have to cut all access to God out of my experience." No, men and women, you cannot approach God on any other ground than the shed blood, and until you believe in the blood of Jesus Christ as a perfect atonement for your sins, and as the only ground on which you can find forgiveness and justification, real prayer is an impossibility.

2. You will find the second part of the answer to the question, How can we come into the presence of God and how can we be sure that we have come into His presence? in Ephesians 2:18, "For through him we both have our access in one Spirit unto the Father." Here we have the same thought that we have already had, that we have just been presenting, that it is "through him," that is, through Jesus Christ, that we have our access to the Father. But we have an additional thought, the thought that when we come into

the presence of God through Jesus Christ, we come "in" the One Spirit, that is, the Holy Spirit. Just what does that mean? It means this: It is the work of the Holy Spirit, when you and I pray, to take us by the hand as it were and lead us into the very presence of God and introduce us to Him, and to make God real to us as we pray. The Greek word translated "access" is the exact equivalent in its etymology of the word "introduction," which is really a Latin word transliterated into English. As I say, it is the work of the Holy Spirit to introduce us to God, that is, to lead us into God's presence, and to make God real to us as we pray (or return thanks, or worship). And in order that we may really come into the presence of God and be sure that we have come into His presence when we pray, we must look to the Holy Spirit to make God real to us while we are praying.

Have you never had this experience, that when you knelt to pray it seemed as if there were no one there, as if you were just talking into the air, or into empty space? What shall we do at such a time as that? Shall we stop praying and wait until some time when we feel like praying? No, when we least feel like praying, and when God is least real to us, that is the time we most need to pray. What shall we do, then? Simply be quiet and look up to God and ask Him to fulfill His promise and send His Holy Spirit to lead us into His presence and to make Him real to us, and then wait and expect. And the Holy Spirit will come, and He will take us into God's presence, and He will make God real to us. I can testify today that some of the most wonderful seasons of prayer I have ever had, have been times when as I first knelt to pray I had no real sense of God. It seemed that no one was there, it seemed as if I were talking into empty space; and then I have just looked up to God and asked Him and trusted Him to send His Holy Spirit to teach me to pray, to lead me into His presence, and to make Him real to me, and the Spirit has come, and He has made God so real to me that it almost seemed that if I opened my eyes I could see Him; in fact, I did see Him with the eyes of my soul.

One night at the close of a sermon in one of the churches on the South Side in Chicago, I went down the aisle to speak to some of the people. I stepped up to a middle-aged man and said to him, "Are you a Christian?" "No," he replied, "I am an infidel. Did you ever see God?" I quickly replied, "Yes, I have seen God." The man was startled and silenced. Did I mean that I had seen God with these eyes of my body? No. But, thank God, I have two pair of eyes; not only does my body have eyes, but my soul also has eyes. I pity the person who has only one pair of eyes, no matter how good those eyes are. I thank God I have two pairs of eyes, these bodily eyes with which I see you, and the eyes of my soul, with which I see God. God has given me wonderful eyes for my body, that at sixty-seven years of age I have never had to wear glasses and do not know what it means to have my eyes weary or painful under any circumstances. But I will gladly give up these eyes rather than those other eyes that God has given me, the eyes with which I see God.

This, then, is the way to come into the presence of God and to be sure that we have come into His presence: first, to come by the blood; second, to come in the Holy Spirit, looking to the Holy Spirit to lead us into the presence of God, and to make God real to us.

In passing, let me call your attention to the great practical importance of the doctrine of the Trinity. Many think that the doctrine of the Trinity is a purely abstract, metaphysical, and utterly impractical doctrine. Not at all. It involves our whole spiritual life, and it is of the highest importance in the very practical matter of praying. We need God the Father to pray to; we need Jesus Christ the Son to pray through; and we need the Holy Spirit to pray in. It is the prayer that is to God the Father, through Jesus Christ the Son, under the guidance and in the power of the Holy Spirit, that God the Father answers.

II. With Intense Earnestness

Now let us consider another of the four phrases used in Acts 12:5 that contain the whole secret of prevailing prayer, the two words "without ceasing"—"Prayer was made without ceasing of the church unto God for him." If you have the Revised Version you will notice that it reads differently, that it reads in this way, "Prayer was made earnestly of the church unto God for him." The word "earnestly" comes far nearer giving the force of the original than the words "without ceasing," but even "earnestly" does not give the full force of the Greek word used. The Greek word is *ektenōs*, which means, literally, "stretched-out-edly." You see how King James' translators came to translate it "without ceasing": they thought of the prayer as stretched out a long time—unceasing prayer. But that is not the thought at all. The Greek word is never used in that sense anywhere in the New Testament, and I do not know of a place in Greek literature outside of the Bible where it is so used. The word is a pictorial word, as so many words are. It represents the soul stretched out in the intensity of its earnestness toward God.

Did you ever see a foot race? The racers are all toeing the mark waiting for the starter to say "Go," or to fire the revolver as a signal to start. As the critical moment approaches, the runners become more and more tense, until when the word "Go" comes, or the revolver cracks, they go racing down the track with every nerve and muscle stretched toward yonder goal, and sometimes the veins stand out on the forehead like whipcords—every runner would be the winner! That is the picture, the soul stretched out in intense earnestness toward God.

It is the same word that is used in the comparative mood in Luke 22:44, which reads, "And being in an agony he prayed more earnestly [literally, more stretched-out-edly]; and his sweat was as it were great drops of blood falling down to the ground." The thought is, as I have said, of the soul being stretched out toward God in intense earnestness of desire.

Probably the most accurate translation that could be given in a single word would be "intensely": "Prayer was made intensely of the church unto God for him." In fact, the word "intensely" is from the same root, but has a different prefix. In the 1911 Bible the passage is translated, "Instant and earnest prayer was made of the church unto God for him," which is not a bad paraphrase, though it is not a translation. And "intensely earnest prayer was made of the church unto God for him" would be an even better rendering.

It is the intensely earnest prayer to which God pays attention, and which He answers. This thought comes out again and again in the Bible. We find it even in the Old Testament, in Jeremiah 29:13, "Ye shall seek me, and find me, when ye shall search for me with all your heart." We here discover the reason why so many of our prayers are unheard of God. There is so little heart in them, so little intensity of desire for the thing asked, that there is no reason why God should pay any attention to them. Suppose I should ask all of you if you prayed this morning. Doubtless almost every one of you would reply, "Yes, I did." Then suppose I should ask you again, "For what did you pray this morning?" I fear that some of you would hesitate and ponder and then have to say, "Really, I forget for what I did pray this morning." Well, then, God will forget to answer. But if I should ask some of you if you prayed this morning you would say, "Yes." Then if I asked you for what you prayed you could tell me at once, for you always pray for the same thing. You have just a little rote of prayer that you go through each morning or each night. You fall on your knees, go through your little prayer automatically, scarcely thinking of what you are saying, in fact, oftentimes you do not think of what you are saying but think of a dozen other things while you are repeating your prayer. Such prayer is profanity, taking the name of God in vain.

When Mrs. Torrey and I were in India, she went up to Darjeeling, in the Himalayas, on the borders of Tibet. I was unable to go because of being so busy with meetings in Calcutta. When she came back she brought with her a Tibetan praying wheel. Did you ever see one? A little round brass cup on the top of a stick; the cup revolves when the stick is whirled. The Tibetan writes out his prayers, drops them into the cup, and then whirls the stick and the wheel goes round and the prayers are said. That is just the way a great many Americans pray, except that the wheel is in their head instead of being on the top of a stick. They kneel down and rattle through a rote of prayer, day after day the same thing, with scarcely any thought of what they are praying for. That kind of prayer is profanity, "taking the name of God in vain," and it has no power whatever with God. It is a pure waste of time, or worse than a waste of time.

But if I should ask some of you what you prayed for this morning you could tell me, for as you were in prayer the Spirit of God came on you, and with a great heartache of intensity of desire you cried to God for that thing you must have. Well, God will hear your prayer and give you what you asked.

If we are to pray with power we must pray with intense earnestness, throw our whole soul into the prayer. This thought comes out again and again in the Bible. For example, we find it in Romans 15:30, "Now I beseech you, brethren, for the Lord Jesus Christ's sake, and for the love of the Spirit, that ye strive together with me in your prayers to God for me." The word translated "strive together" in this verse is *sunagonizo*. *Agonizo* means to "contend" or "strive" or "wrestle" or "fight." And this verse could be properly translated, "Now I beseech you, brethren, for the Lord Jesus Christ's sake, and for the love of the Spirit, that ye wrestle together with me in your prayers to God for me."

We hear a great deal these days about "the rest of faith," by which men usually mean that we should take things very calmly in our Christian life, and when we pray we simply come into God's presence like a little child and quietly and trustfully ask Him for the thing desired and count it ours, and go away very calmly, and reckon the thing ours. Now, there is a truth in that, a great truth; but it is only one side of the truth, and a truth usually has two sides. And the other side of the truth is this, that there is not only "the rest of faith" but there is also the "fight of faith," and my Bible has more to say about "the fight of faith" than it has about "the rest of faith." The thought of wrestling or fighting in prayer is not the thought that we have to wrestle with God to make God willing to grant our prayers. No, "our wrestling is . . . against the principalities, against the powers, against the world rulers of this darkness, against the spiritual hosts of wickedness in the heavenly places" (Eph. 6:12), against the devil and all his mighty forces, and there is no place where the devil so resists us as when we pray. Sometimes when we pray it seems as if all the forces of hell sweep in between us and God. What shall we do? Give up? No! A thousand times, no! Fight the thing through on your knees, wrestle in your prayer to God, and win.

Some years ago I was attending a Bible conference in Dr. James H. Brooks' old church in St. Louis. On the program was one of the most distinguished and most gifted Bible teachers that America ever produced, and he was speaking this day on "The Rest of Faith." He said, "I challenge anybody to show me a single passage in the Bible where we are told to wrestle in prayer." Now one speaker does not like to contradict another, but here was a challenge, and I was sitting on the platform, and I was obliged to take it up. So I said in a low tone of voice, "Romans 15:30, brother." He was a good enough Greek scholar to know that I had him, and what is more rare, he was honest enough to own it up on the spot. Yes, the Bible bids us "wrestle in prayer," and it is the prayer in which we actually wrestle in the power of the Holy Spirit that wins with God. The root of the word translated "strive together" is *agōnē*, from which our word "agony" comes. In fact, in Luke 22:44, to which I have already referred, this is the very word that is translated "agony," "And being in an agony he prayed more earnestly: and his sweat was as it were great drops of blood falling to the ground." Oh that we might have more agonizing prayer.

Turn now to Colossians 4:12, 13, and you will find the same thought again, put in other words, "Epaphras, who is one of you, a servant of Christ, saluteth you, always labouring fervently for you [The Revised Version has it "laboring fervently for you" instead of "striving for you," the same word we saw in Rom. 15:30] in prayers, that ye may stand perfect and complete in all the will of God. For I bear him record, that he hath a great zeal for you." The words translated "great zeal" in this version are translated in the Revised Version, "much labor," which is an accurate translation. The word translated "labour" is a very strong word; it means intense toil, or, painful labor. Do you know what it means to toil in prayer, to labor with painful toil in prayer? Oh, how easily most of us take our praying, how little heart we put into it, and how little it takes out of us, and how little it counts with God.

The mighty men of God who throughout the centuries have wrought great things by prayer are the men who have had much painful toil in prayer. Take, for example, David Brainerd, that physically feeble but spiritual mighty man of God. Trembling for years on the verge of consumption, from which he ultimately died at an early age, David Brainerd felt led of God to labor among the North American Indians in the early days, in the primeval forests of northern Pennsylvania, and sometimes of a winter night he would go out into the forest and kneel in the cold snow when it was a foot deep and so labor with God in prayer that he would be wringing wet with perspiration even out in the cold winter-night hours. And God heard David Brainerd and sent such a mighty revival among the North American Indians as had never been heard of before, as, indeed, had never been dreamed of. And not only did God send in answer to David Brainerd's prayers this mighty revival among the North American Indians, but also in answer to David Brainerd's prayers he transformed David Brainerd's father-in-law, Jonathan Edwards, that mighty prince of metaphysicians, probably the mightiest thinker that America has ever produced (the only American metaphysician whose name is in the American Hall of Fame), into Jonathan Edwards the flaming evangelist, who so preached on the subject of "Sinners in the Hands of an Angry God," in the church at Enfield, in the power of the Holy Spirit, that the strong men in the audience felt as if the very floor of the church were falling out and they were sinking into hell, and they sprang to their feet and threw their arms around the pillars of the church and cried to God for mercy. Oh that we had more men who could pray like David Brainerd, then we would have more men that could preach like Jonathan Edwards.

I once used this illustration of David Brainerd at a conference in New York State. Dr. Park, the grandson and biographer of Jonathan Edwards, who was in my audience, came to me at the close and said, "I have always felt that there was something abnormal about David Brainerd." I replied, "Doctor Park, it would be a good thing for you and a good thing for me if we had a little more of that kind of abnormality." Indeed it would, and it would be a good thing if many of us who are here this morning had that kind of so-called "abnormality" that bows a man down with intensity of longing for the power of God, that would make us pray in the way that David Brainerd prayed.

But a very practical question arises at this point. How can we get this intense earnestness in prayer? The Bible answers the question very plainly and simply. There are two ways of having earnestness in prayer, a right way and a wrong way. The wrong way is to work it up in the energy of the flesh. Have you never seen it done? A man kneels down by a chair to pray; he begins very calmly and then he begins to work himself up and begins to shout and scream and pound the chair, and sometimes he spits foam, and he screams until your head is almost splitting with the loud uproar. That is the wrong way, that is false fire; that is the energy of the flesh, which is an abomination to God. If possible, that is even worse than the careless, thoughtless prayers of which I have spoken.

But there is a right way to obtain real, heart-stirring, heart-wringing, and God-moving earnestness in prayer. What the right way is the Bible tells us. It tells us in Romans 8:26, 27, R.V., "And in like manner the Spirit also helpeth our infirmity; for we know not how to pray as we ought; but the Spirit himself maketh intercession for us with groanings which cannot be uttered, and he that searcheth the hearts knoweth what is the mind of the Spirit, because he maketh intercession for the saints according to the will of God." That is the right way—look to the Spirit to create the earnestness. The earnestness that counts with God is not the earnestness that you or I work up; it is the earnestness that the Holy Spirit creates in our hearts. Have you never gone to God in prayer and there was no earnestness in your prayer at all, it was just words, words, words, a mere matter of form, when it seemed there was no real prayer in your heart? What shall we do at such a time as that? Stop praying and wait until we feel more like praying? No. If there is ever a time when one needs to pray it is when he does not feel like praying. What shall we do? Be silent and look up to God to send His Holy Spirit, according to His promise, to move your heart to prayer and to awaken and create real earnestness in your heart in prayer: and God will send Him and you will pray with intense earnestness, very likely "with groanings which cannot be uttered."

I wish to testify right here that some of the times of deepest earnestness that I have ever known in prayer came when at the outset I seemed to have no prayer in my heart at all, and all attempt to pray was mere words, words, empty form. And then I looked up to God to send His Spirit according to His promise to teach me to pray, and I waited and the Spirit of God came on me in mighty power and I cried to God, sometimes with groanings which could not be uttered.

I shall never forget a night in Chicago. After the general prayer meetings for a world-wide revival had been going on for some time, the man who was most closely associated with me in the conduct of the meetings came over to my house one night after the meeting was over and said, "Brother Torrey, what do you say to our having a time alone with God every Saturday night after the other meetings are over? I do not mean," he continued, "that we will actually promise to come together every Saturday night; but let us have it tonight, anyway." Oh, such a night of prayer as we had that night. I shall never forget that, but it was not that night that I am especially thinking of now. After we had been meeting some weeks, he suggested that we invite in a few others, which we did; and every Saturday night after the general prayer meeting was closed at ten o'clock we few would gather in some secluded place where we would not disturb others to pray together. There were never more than a dozen persons present; usually there were six or seven. One night, before kneeling in prayer, we told one another the things we desired especially to ask of God that night, and then we knelt to pray and a long silence followed. No one prayed. And one of the little company looked up and said, "I cannot pray, there seems to be something resisting me." Then another raised his head and said, "Neither can I pray, something seems to be resisting me." We went around the whole circle, and each one had the same story.

What did we do? Break up the prayer meeting? No. If ever we felt the need of prayer it was then, and quietly we all bowed before God and looked to Him to send His Holy Spirit to enable us to pray to victory. And soon the Spirit of God came on one and another, and I have seldom heard such praying as I heard that night. And then the Spirit of God came on me and led me out in such a prayer as I had never dreamed of praying. I was led to ask God that He would send me around the world preaching the Gospel, and give me to see thousands saved in China, in Japan, in Australia, in New Zealand, in Tasmania, in India, in England, Scotland, Ireland, Germany, France, and Switzerland; and when I finished praying that night I knew I was going, and I knew what I would see as well as I knew afterward when the actual report came of the mighty things that God had wrought. That prayer meeting sent me around the world preaching the Gospel.

Oh, that is how we must pray if we would get what we ask in prayer—pray with the intense earnestness that the Holy Ghost alone can inspire.

III. Of the Church

Now let us look briefly at another one of the four phrases, the phrase "of the church." The prayer that God particularly delights to answer is united prayer. There is power in the prayer of a single individual, and the prayer of individuals has wrought great things, but there is far greater power in united prayer. Our Lord Jesus taught this same great truth in Matthew 8:19, 20, "Again I say unto you, that if two of you shall agree on earth as touching anything that they shall ask, it shall be done for them of my Father who is in heaven." God delights in the unity of His people, and He does everything in His power to promote that unity, and so He especially honors unity in prayer. There is power in the prayer of one true believer: there is far more power in the united prayer of two, and greater power in the united prayer of still more.

But it must be real unity. This comes out in the exact words our Lord uses. He says, "If two of you shall agree on earth as touching anything that they shall ask, it shall be done for them of my Father who is in heaven." It is one of the most frequently misquoted and most constantly abused promises in the whole Bible. It is often quoted as if it read this way, "Again I say unto you, that if two of you shall agree on earth to ask anything, it shall be done for them of my Father who is in heaven." But it actually reads, "Again I say unto you, that if two of you shall agree on earth as touching anything that they shall ask, it shall be done for them of my Father who is in heaven." Someone may say, "I do not see any essential difference." Let me explain it to you. Someone else has a burden on his heart, he comes to you and asks you to unite with him in praying for deliverance and you consent, and you both pray for it. Now you are "agreed" in praying, but you are not agreed at all "as touching" what you ask. He asks for it because he intensely desires it; you ask for it simply because he asks you to ask for it. You are not at all agreed "as touching" what you ask. But when God, by His Holy Spirit, puts the same burden on two hearts, and they thus in the unity of the Spirit pray for the same thing, there is not power enough on earth or in hell to keep them from getting it. Our Heavenly Father will do for them the thing that they ask.

IV. "For Him"

Now let us look at the fourth phrase, "for him." The prayer was definite prayer for a definite person; and that is the kind of prayer God answers, *definite prayer*. Oh how general and vague many of our prayers are. They are very pretty, they sound nice, they are charmingly phrased, but they ask no definite, specific thing, and they get no definite, specific answer. When you pray to God, have a very definite, clear-cut idea of just exactly what it is you want of God, and ask Him for that definite and specific thing; and, if you meet the other conditions of prevailing prayer, you will get that definite, specific thing which you asked. God's answer will be just as definite as your prayer.

In closing, let me call your attention to our dependence on the Holy Spirit in all our praying if we are to accomplish anything by our prayers. It is the Holy Spirit, as we saw in our study of the first phrase, who enables us really to pray "unto God," who leads us into the presence of God and makes God real to us. It is the Holy Spirit, again, who gives us the intense earnestness in prayer that prevails with God. Still again, it is the Holy Spirit who brings us into unity so that we know the power of really united prayer. And it is the Holy Spirit who shows us the definite things for which we should definitely pray.

To sum it all up, the prayer that God answers is the prayer that is to God the Father, that is on the ground of the atoning blood of God the Son, and that is under the direction and in the power of God the Holy Spirit.

VII. The Great Attraction

And I, if I be lifted up from the earth, will draw all men unto myself.

JOHN 12:32, R.V.

IN A RECENT advertisement of a Sunday evening service in one of our American cities it was stated that there would be three attractions: a high-class movie show, a popular gospel pianist and his wife, and an aria from the opera, "Madame Butterfly," rendered by a well-known prima donna. It is somewhat startling when an unusually gifted and popular preacher, or his advertising committee, thinks of the Gospel of the Son of God as having so lost its power to draw that it must be bolstered up by putting on a selection from a very questionable opera, rendered by a professional opera singer, as an additional attraction to help out our once-crucified and now-glorified Saviour and Lord.

This advertisement set me to thinking as to what really was the great attraction to men in this day as well as in former days. At once there came to my mind the words of our text containing God's answer to this question: "And I, if I be lifted up from the earth, will draw all men unto myself." There is nothing else that draws like the uplifted Christ. Movies may get a crowd of empty-headed and empty-hearted young men and maidens, and even middle-aged folks without brains or moral earnestness, for a time, but nothing really draws and holds the men and women who are worth while like Jesus Christ lifted up. Nineteen centuries of Christian history prove the drawing power of Jesus when He is properly presented to men. I have seen some wonderful verifications of the assertion of our text as to the marvelous drawing power of the uplifted Christ.

In London, for two continuous months, six afternoons and evenings each week, I saw the great Royal Albert Hall filled and even jammed, and sometimes as many turned away as got in, though it would seat ten thousand people by actual count and stand two thousand more in the dome. On the opening night of these meetings a leading reporter of the city of London came to me before the service began and said, "You have taken this building for two consecutive months?" "Yes." "And you expect to fill it every day?" "Yes." "Why," he said, "no one has ever attempted to hold two weeks' consecutive meetings here of any kind. Gladstone himself could not fill it for two weeks. And you really expect to fill it for two months?" I replied, "Come and see." He came and he saw.

On the last night, when the place was jammed to its utmost capacity and thousands outside clamored for admission, he came to me again, and I said, "Has it been filled?" He smiled and said, "It has." But what filled it? No show on earth could have filled it once a day for many consecutive days. The preacher was no remarkable orator. He had no gift of wit and humor, and would not have exercised it if he had. The newspapers constantly called attention to the fact that he was no orator, but the crowds came and came and came; rainy days, and fine days they crowded in or stood outside, oftentimes in a downpour of rain, in the vain hope of getting in. *What drew them?* The uplifted Christ preached and sung in the power of the Holy Ghost, given in answer to the daily prayers of forty thousand people scattered throughout the earth.

In Liverpool, the Tournament Hall, that was said to seat twenty thousand people, and that by actual count seated 12,500 comfortably, located in a very out-of-the-way part of the city, several blocks from the nearest street-car line, and perhaps half a mile from all the regular street-car lines, was filled night after night for three months, and on the last night they crowded fifteen thousand people into the building at seven o'clock, and then emptied it, and crowded another fifteen thousand in who had been patiently waiting outside—30,000 people drawn in a single night! By what? By whom? Not by the preacher, not by the singer, but by Him who had said nearly nineteen hundred years before, "And I, if I be lifted up from the earth, will draw all men unto myself."

I. The Exact Meaning of the Text

Let us now look at the exact meaning of the text.

1. First, notice who is the speaker, and what were the circumstances under which He spoke? The Speaker was our Lord Jesus. Not the Christ of men's imaginings, but the Christ of reality, the Christ of actual historic fact. Not the Christ of Mary Baker Eddy's maudlin fancy, or of Madam Besant's mystical imaginings, but the Christ of actuality, who lived here among men and was seen, heard, and handled by men, and who was seen to die a real death to save real sinners from a real hell for a real heaven.

The circumstances were these. Certain Greeks among those who went up to worship at the Jewish feast came to one of the apostles, Philip, and said, "We would see Jesus." And Philip went to Andrew and told Andrew what these

Greeks had said. Andrew and Philip together came and told Jesus. In the heart-cry of these Greeks, "We would see Jesus," our Lord recognized the yearning of the universal heart, the heart of Greek, as well as of Jew, for a satisfying Saviour. The Greeks had their philosophers and sages, their would-be satisfiers and saviours, the greatest the world has ever known, Socrates, Aristotle, Plato, Epictetus, Epimenides, and many others; but they did not save, and they did not satisfy, and the Greeks cried, "We would see Jesus"; and in their eager coming Jesus foresaw the millions of all nations who would flock to Him when He had been crucified as the universal Saviour, meeting all the needs of all mankind, and so He cried, "And I, if I be lifted up from the earth, will draw all men unto myself."

2. In the second place, notice the words, "If I be lifted up." To what does Jesus refer? The next verse answers the question. "But this he said, signifying by what manner of death he should die." Jesus referred to His lifting up on the cross, to die as an atoning Saviour for all mankind. This verse is often quoted as if it meant that, if we lifted up Christ in our preaching, He would draw men. That is true, and it is a crying shame that we do not more often hold up only Him in our preaching, for we would draw far more people if we did. But that is not our Lord's meaning. The lifting up clearly referred, not to His not being lifted up in our preaching, but to His being lifted up on the cross by His enemies to expose Him to awful shame and to an agonizing death. It is Christ crucified who draws, it is Christ crucified who meets the deepest needs of the heart of all mankind; it is an atoning Saviour, a Saviour who atones for the sins of men by His death, and thus saves from the holy wrath of an infinitely holy God,

who meets the needs of men, and thus draws all men, for all men are sinners. Preach any Christ but a crucified Christ, and you will not draw men for long. Preach any gospel but a gospel of atoning blood, and it will not draw for long.

Unitarianism does not draw men. Unitarian churches are born only to die. Their corpses strew New England today. Many of their ministers have been intellectually among the most brilliant our country has ever known, but their churches even under scholarly and brilliant ministers die, die, die! Why? Because Unitarianism presents a gospel without atoning blood, and Jesus has said and history has proven it true, "And I, if I be lifted up from the earth, will draw all men unto myself." "Christian Science," strangely so called, for, as has been often truly said, "it is neither Christian nor scientific," draws crowds of men and women of a certain type, men and women who have or imagine that they have physical ailments, and who will follow anything, no matter how absurd, that promises them a little surcease from their real or imagined pains. It also draws crowds who wish to fancy that they have some religion without paying the price of true religion, genuine love, real self-sacrifice, and costly sympathy. But Christian Science does not draw all men, that is, all kinds and conditions and ranks of men. In fact, for the most part, it does not draw men at all, but women, and the alleged men it draws are for the most part women in trousers, and men who see an easy way to make a living by preying on the credulity of luckless females. No, a bloodless gospel, a gospel with a Christ but not a Christ lifted up on a cross, does not meet the universal needs of men, and so does not draw all men.

Congregationalism of late years has been sadly tinctured

with Unitarianism. In spite of the fact that it has been an eyewitness to Unitarianism's steady decay and death, Congregationalism has largely dropped the atoning blood out of its theology, and consequently it is rapidly going to the wall. Its once-great Andover Seminary, still great in the size of its endowment given for the teaching of Bible orthodoxy, but which the conscienceless teachers of a bloodless theology have deliberately taken for the exploitation of their "damnable heresies" (II Pet. 2:1), and which is still great in the number of its professors, graduated at their annual exercises last spring just three men, one a Japanese, one a Hindu, and one an American. A theology without a crucified Saviour, without the atoning blood, won't draw. It does not meet the need. No, no, the words of our Lord are still true, "And I, if I be lifted up from the earth, will draw all men unto myself."

3. Note, in the third place, the words, "Draw all men." Does "all men" mean all individuals or men of all races? Did Jesus mean that every man and woman who lived on this earth would be drawn to Him, or did He mean that men of all races would be drawn to Him? The context answers the question. The Greeks, as we have seen, came to one of the apostles, Philip, and said, "We would see Jesus," and Philip had gone and told Andrew, and Andrew and Philip had gone and told Jesus. Our Lord's ministry during His earthly life was to Jews only, and in the coming of these Greeks so soon before His death our Lord saw the presage of the coming days when by His death on the cross the barrier between Jews and Gentiles would be broken down and all nations would have their opportunity equally with the Jews, when by His atoning death on the cross men of all nations would be drawn to Him. He did not say that He would draw every individual, but all races

of men, Greeks as well as Jews, Romans, Scythians, French, English, Germans, Japanese, Americans, and men of all nations. He is a universal Saviour, and true Christianity is a universal religion. Mohammedanism, Buddhism, Confucianism, and all religions but Christianity, are religions of a restricted application. Christianity, with a crucified Christ as its center, is a universal religion and meets the needs of all mankind. It meets the needs of the European as well as the needs of the Asiatic, the needs of the Occident as well as the needs of the Orient, the needs of the American Indian and the needs of the African Negro; and so our Lord said, "And I, if I be lifted up from the earth, will draw all men unto myself."

No race has ever been found anywhere on this earth to which the Gospel did not appeal and whose deepest need the crucified Christ did not meet. Many years ago, when Charles Darwin, the eminent English scientist, came in contact with the Terre del Fuegans in their gross degradation, he publicly declared that here was a people to whom it was vain to send missionaries, as the Gospel could not do anything for them. But brave men of God went there and took the Gospel to them in the power of the Holy Spirit, and demonstrated that it met the need of the Terre del Fuegans, with such great results that Charles Darwin publicly admitted his mistake and became a regular subscriber to the work.

The Gospel, with a crucified Christ as its center, meets the needs of all conditions and classes of men as well as of all races. It meets the need of the millionaire and the need of the pauper; it meets the need of great men of science like James D. Dana and Lord Kelvin, and the need of the man or woman who cannot read or write; it meets the need of the king on the throne and the need of the laborer in the ditch. I myself have seen with my own eyes noblemen and servant girls, university deans and men who could scarcely read, prisoners in penitentiaries and leaders in moral uplift, brilliant lawyers and dull, plodding workingmen, come under its attraction, and be saved by its power. But it was only because I made "Christ crucified," His atoning work, the center of my preaching.

4. Notice, in the fourth place, the words, "unto me." "I will draw all men unto me." The Revised Version reads "unto myself," and that was just what Jesus said, "And I, if I be lifted up from the earth, will draw all men unto myself." It is not to a creed or a system of doctrine that Jesus draws men, but to a Person, to Himself. That is what we need, a Person, Jesus Himself. As He Himself once said, "Come unto me, all ye that labour and are heavy laden, and I will give you rest" (Matt. 11:28). Creeds and confessions of faith are all right in their place, they are of great value; the organized church is of great value, it is indispensable, and it is the most important institution in the world today. Society would soon go to rack and ruin without it; we are all under solemn obligation to God and to our fellow man to support it and belong to it; but creeds and confessions of faith cannot save; the church cannot save; a Divine Person can save, Jesus Christ, and He alone. So He says, "And I, if I be lifted up from the earth, will draw all men unto myself."

II. Why Christ Lifted Up on the Cross Draws All Men unto Himself

But why does Christ lifted up on the cross, the crucified Christ, draw all men unto Himself? There are two reasons why Christ lifted up, and Christ crucified, draws all men unto Himself.

1. First of all, Christ crucified draws all men unto Himself because Christ crucified meets the first, the deepest, the greatest and most fundamental need of man. What is man's first, greatest, deepest, most fundamental need? A Saviour? A Saviour from what? First of all, and underlying all else, a Saviour from the guilt of sin. Every man of every race has sinned. As Paul put it in Romans 3:23, "There is no difference, for all have sinned and come short of the glory of God." There is no difference between Jew and Gentile at this point, nor is there any difference between English and German at this point; there is no difference between American and Japanese at this point, no difference between European and Asiatic, no difference between the American and the African. "There is no difference; for all have sinned and come short of the glory of God." Every man of every race is a sinner; "there is no difference" at this point. And every man will have to answer for his sin to the infinitely holy God who rules this universe. Therefore, all men need an atoning Saviour, who can by His atoning death make propitiation for, and so cover up, our sins, and thus reconcile us to this holy God, and deliver us from His awful wrath, and bring us out into the glorious sunlight of His favor. And Jesus lifted up is the only atoning Saviour in the universe. He who alone was at the same time God and man, He alone can make atonement for sin; and He has made it, has made a perfect atonement, and God has accepted His atonement and testified to His acceptance of His atonement by raising Him from the dead. The Lord Jesus actually meets our need, He actually meets every man's first, greatest, deepest, most fundamental need, and He alone. In all the universe there is no religion but Christianity that even offers an atoning Saviour. Mohammedanism offers Mohammed,

"The Prophet," a teacher, but not a Saviour; Buddhism offers Buddha, supposedly at least a wonderful teacher, "The Light of Asia," but not an atoning Saviour; Confucianism offers Confucius, a marvelous teacher far ahead of his time, but not an atoning Saviour. No religion but Christianity offers an atoning Saviour, an atonement of any real character. This is the radical point of difference between Christianity and every other religion in the world, yet some fool preachers are trying to eliminate from Christianity this supreme fact, its very point of radical difference from all other religions. But such an emasculated Christianity will not reach the needs of men and will not draw men. It never has and it never will. The Bible and history are at one on this. Jesus Christ offers Himself lifted up on the cross to redeem us from the curse of the law by "becoming a curse in our behalf." "Christ hath redeemed us from the curse of the law, being made a curse for us; for it is written, Cursed is every one that hangeth on a tree" (Gal. 3:13). Men know their need; they may try to forget it, they may try to deny it; they may try to drown their sense of it by drink and dissipation or by wild pleasure-seeking or wild money-getting, or by listening to fake preachers in supposedly orthodox pulpits, like one who in this city declared recently that "the old sense of sin is fast disappearing," and added, "The change is for the better, not for the worse." He spoke also of "imaginary and artificial sins like 'the sin of unbelief,'" and then went on to say, "In this we agree with Christ," apparently not knowing enough about the Bible to know that Jesus Himself was the very one who said in John 16:8, 9, "And he, when he is come, will convict the world in respect of sin, and of righteousness, and of judgment; of sin, because they believe not on me."

But in spite of all our attempts to drown or stupefy or silence our sense of sin, our consciousness of guilt before a Holy God, we all have it, and, like Banquo's ghost, it will not drown. Nothing gives the guilty conscience abiding peace but the atoning blood of Jesus Christ. And so Christ lifted up draws all men unto Him, and even wicked ministers of Satan, like the preacher I have just referred to, sometimes come to their senses and flee to the real Christ, Christ crucified, as I hope this one may. Yes, Jesus, Jesus only, Jesus lifted up on the cross, Jesus crucified for our sins, making full atonement for our sins, He and He alone meets the deepest need of us all, and so His cross draws us all unto Himself. Happy the man or the woman who yields to that drawing. Woe be to the man or woman who resists that drawing; final gloom, despondency, and despair are their lot. Oh, how many men and women who have gotten their eyes opened to see the facts, to see their awful guilt, and who have been plunged into deepest consequent despair, have come to me, and I have pointed them to Jesus on the cross, and have shown them by God's Word all their sins laid upon Him and thus settled, and they have come to Him, and believed God's testimony about Him, that He had borne all their sins in His own body on the cross, and they have found perfect peace and boundless joy. And that is the only way to find perfect peace and boundless joy.

Will you set out to find peace? If you do not, great gloom, utter despair, awaits you some day, in this world or in the world to come. In my first pastorate I tried to get a man to come to Christ lifted up to meet his need of pardon; but though it was many years ago he held to the theology that is preached as "new theology" today, and sought to still the voice of conscience, and stupefy his sense of sin by denying his guilt and his need of an atoning Saviour. He did not wish to listen to me nor to see me. But the hour came when death drew nigh. A cancer was eating its way through scalp and skull into his brain; then he cried to those about his dying bed, "Send for Mr. Torrey." I hurried to his side. He was in despair. "Oh!" he said, "Dr. Tidhall tells me that I have but a short time to live, that as soon as this cancer gets a little farther and eats through the thin film of skull and touches the brain I am a dead man. Tell me how to be saved." I sat down beside him, and told him what to do to be saved. I tried to make as plain as I knew how the way of salvation through the uplifted Christ, Christ uplifted on the cross, and I think I know how to make it plain, but he had waited too long, he could not grasp it. I stayed with him. Night came on. I said to his family, "You have been up night after night with him, I will sit with him tonight." They instructed me what to do, how to minister to him. Time after time during the night I had to go to another room to get some nourishment for him, and as I would come back into the room where he lay, from his bed in the corner there would rise the constant cry, "Oh, I wish I were a Christian. Oh, I wish I were a Christian. Oh, I wish I were a Christian." And thus he died.

2. In the second place, Christ lifted up on the cross, Christ crucified, draws all men unto Him, because lifted up there to die for us He reveals His wonderful love, and the wondrous love of the Father for us. "Hereby know we the love of God, because he laid down his life for us" (I John 3:16), and "God commendeth his love toward us, in that while we were yet sinners, Christ died for us" (Rom. 5:6, 8). There is nothing that draws men like love. Love draws all men of every clime. But no love draws like

the love of God. "For God so loved the world that he gave his only begotten son, that whosoever believeth in him should not perish, but have everlasting life" (John 3:16) has broken thousands of hard hearts.

One night, preaching in my own church in Minneapolis, the whole choir stayed for the after-meeting. The leading soprano was an intelligent young woman but living a worldly life. She remained with the rest. In the after-meeting her mother arose in the back of the church and said, "I wish you would pray for the conversion of my daughter." I did not look around but knew instinctively that the daughter's cheeks were flushing, and her eyes flashing with anger. As soon as the meeting was dismissed, I hurried down so that I would meet her before she got out of the church. As she came toward me I held out my hand to her. She stamped her foot, and with flashing eyes cried, "Mr. Torrey, my mother knows better than to do that. She knows it will only make me worse." I said, "Sit down, Cora." She sat down, and without any argument I opened my Bible to Isaiah 53:5, and began to read, "But he was wounded for our transgressions; he was bruised for our iniquities; the chastisement of our peace was upon him; and with his stripes we are healed." She burst into tears, and the next night accepted Jesus Christ. I had to go to Duluth for a few days, and when I returned I found that she was seriously ill. One morning her brother came hurrying up to my home and said that she was apparently dying, that she was unconscious, and white from the loss of blood. I hastened down, and as I entered the room she lay there with her eyes closed, with the whitest face I ever saw on one who was not actually dead. She was apparently unconscious, scarcely breathing. I knelt by her side to pray, more for the sake of the mother who stood beside the bed than for her, for I supposed that she was beyond help or hearing. But no sooner had I finished my prayer than in a clear, full, richly musical tone she began to pray. These were about her words, "Heavenly Father, if it be Thy will, raise me up that as I have used my voice for myself and only to please myself I may use my voice for Thy glory, but if in Thy wisdom Thou seest that it is best for me not to live, I shall be glad to go to be with Christ," and she went to be with Christ.

Oh, I have seen thousands melted as I have repeated to them and shown them the picture of Christ on the cross, as told in Isaiah 53:5, "But he was wounded for our transgressions; he was bruised for our iniquities; the chastisement of our peace was upon him; and with his stripes we are healed."

A few days ago I received a missionary magazine containing a testimony from one who was going to Egypt under the Egypt General Mission. This young missionary said, "When I was twelve years old, during the Torrey-Alexander meetings, in 1904, I gave my heart to the Lord Jesus Christ. Dr. Torrey was speaking on the text, Isaiah 53:5, and he asked us to repeat the words with him, but changing the word 'our' into the word 'my.' While repeating the text in this way I suddenly realized, as if for the first time, that Jesus had really suffered all this for me, and there and then I gave my life to Him."

Oh, men and women, look now! See Jesus Christ lifted up on the cross, see Him hanging on that awful cross, see Him wounded for your transgressions, bruised for your iniquities, and the chastisement of your peace laid on Him. Oh, men and women living in sin, men and women rejecting Christ for the world, men and women who have looked to the lies of other systems that deny His atoning blood, listen! "But he was wounded for our transgressions; he was bruised for our iniquities; the chastisement of our peace was upon him; and with his stripes we are healed." Won't you yield to that love, won't you give up your sin, give up your worldly pleasures, give up your willful errors, and accept the Saviour who loves you, and died for you, who was "wounded for your transgressions; bruised for your iniquities" and upon whom the chastisement of your peace was laid? Accept Him right now!

VIII. The Most Important Question

What shall I do then with Jesus which is called Christ?
MATTHEW 27:22.

IF I SHOULD PUT to this audience tonight the question, What is the most important question of the day, I presume I would get a great variety of answers. Some of you would say that the disarmament question or the Four Power Treaty question was the most important question of the day. Some would say that the labor question was the most important question of the day. And still others would say that the Prohibition question was the most important question of the day, and so on. But all these answers would be wrong. There is another question of vastly more importance than any one of these, a question of the right decision on which immeasurably more depends than on the decision of any of these questions. That question is this, "What shall I do with Jesus, which is called Christ?"

It is not a new question. Pontius Pilate asked it nearly nineteen hundred years ago, and answered it wrong, and his earthly life went out in darkness, and his eternity was blasted. Thousands on thousands have asked it since. On a right decision of that question everything that is really worth having for time and for eternity depends for each one of us. If you do the right thing with Jesus, the Christ of God, you will get everything that is really worth hav-

121

ing for time as well as for eternity, whether a right decision is given on these various other questions or not. If you do the wrong thing with Jesus, the Christ of God, you will lose everything that is worth having for time as well as for eternity, even though all these other questions are decided as they should be.

1. What We Will Get if We Do the Right Thing with Jesus Christ

Let us look at some of the things that we will get if we do the right thing with Jesus Christ.

1. In the first place, if you do the right thing with Jesus you will get the forgiveness of all your sins. Saint Peter says in Acts 10:43, "To him bear all the prophets witness, that through his name every one that believeth on him shall receive remission of sins." Now this statement is as plain as day, and in it God's inspired apostle declares that "every one that believeth on" Jesus Christ "shall receive remission of [his] sins." If the vilest sinner on earth should come in here tonight and should put his trust in Jesus Christ, the moment he did it all his sins would be forgiven, blotted out.

The forgiveness of our sins depends solely on what we do with Jesus Christ. It does not depend on our prayers or on our penances or on our good works. If you do the right thing with Jesus Christ you get forgiveness of all your sins, whatever else you may do or not do. If you do the wrong thing with Jesus Christ you will not get forgiveness of sins, whatever else you may do or not do. The same truth is put in a different way in John 3:18, "He that believeth on him is not condemned; but he that believeth not is condemned already, because he hath not believed in the name of the only begotten Son of God."

What an unspeakable blessing the forgiveness of all your sins is. Wealth, honors, pleasures, are not so eagerly to be desired as the forgiveness of our sins. All of them together are not to be compared with the forgiveness of our sins. Forgiveness of sin brings joy anywhere it comes, whether it be into the palace or into the prison cell. King David had wealth, honor, power, pleasures, and privileges without number, but he was not happy. Indeed, he was perfectly miserable. His own description of his condition is found in the Thirty-second Psalm, the third and fourth verses; "When I kept silence, my bones waxed old through my roaring all the day long. For day and night thy hand was heavy upon me: my moisture is turned into the drought of summer." Then he found forgiveness of sin and in his joy he shouted, "Blessed is he whose transgression is forgiven, whose sin is covered. Blessed is the man unto whom Jehovah imputeth not iniquity" (Ps. 32:1, 2).

Down in a wretched cell in Sing Sing Prison there was a man under a fifteen-year sentence for manslaughter. He was, of course, a very unhappy man. But there in his cell he got hold of a Bible and read it, and through the Bible the Holy Spirit showed him the Lord Jesus as his Saviour who died in his place, and he accepted Jesus Christ as his Saviour. It was in the middle of the night when he finally found the Saviour through meditating on what he had read in the Word of God, and though it was in the middle of the night and in a prison cell, such joy came into his soul that he began to shout. The guard came along and rapped on his door and told him to keep still. "I can't keep still," he shouted back, "my sins are forgiven." Yes, there is a more wonderful joy in knowing that our sins are all forgiven than there is in anything that this world has to give.

And *we get this forgiveness of sin by simply believing on the Lord Jesus Christ.*

2. In the second place, you will get peace of conscience by doing the right thing with Jesus Christ. It is a blessed thing to have a conscience that does not accuse you, a conscience that has found perfect peace. It is an awful thing to have a conscience that does accuse. It is the greatest misery on earth. It drives many men and many women to suicide. Oh, in what agony of mind men and women have come to me from different ranks of society because of an accusing conscience. And there are many who never unburden their hearts to others who are in misery from the same cause. There are men and women here tonight who spend days and nights of misery because of an accusing conscience. You try to drown the voice of conscience in many ways, but you fail utterly. You try to drown the voice of conscience in pleasure and dissipation. You try to drown the voice of conscience in business. You try to drown the voice of conscience in drink and in dope, and in other ways; but you do not succeed. You never will succeed.

One who perhaps knows as much about the life of the movie colony in Hollywood as anyone else told a friend of mine a few weeks ago of two of the leading stars in the movie world, two women whose names are constantly in the daily papers and who are admired and envied by thousands, that they were the hopeless slaves of dope, and all over this land people who are counted gifted, and on whom others look in envy, are trying to silence the voice of conscience by dope. But no one ever yet found real peace in that way, and no one ever will. Jesus Christ alone can give the guilty conscience peace. In Romans 5:1, God put it through the Apostle Paul in this way, "Being justified by faith, we have peace with God through our Lord Jesus Christ." Do the right thing with Jesus Christ and you will get true peace of conscience, deep, abiding peace, perfect peace. As Isaiah puts it, "Thou wilt keep him in perfect peace, whose mind is stayed on thee: because he trusteth in thee" (26:3). But do the wrong thing with Jesus Christ, and you cannot find peace of conscience in this world or in the next, no matter what else you may do to get peace.

I was dealing once in my office with a woman who told me that she had been in a perfect hell for fourteen years because of an accusing conscience. I pointed her to Jesus Christ. I showed her from God's Word how all her sins had been laid on Jesus Christ. She believed it. She took God's Word for it, put her trust in Him as her atoning Saviour. After fourteen years of agony, of hell on earth, she went out from my office that day with a radiant countenance, for she had found peace of conscience in the only way in which peace of conscience can ever be found by anybody, through her Lord Jesus Christ. And that joy continues until this day.

3. In the third place, you will get deliverance from the power of sin by doing the right thing with Jesus Christ. It is a dreadful thing to be in the power of sin. There is no other slavery so binding, so degrading, and so crushing as the slavery of sin. We all know what a dreadful thing it is to be in the power of some sins. We all know, for example, what an awful thing it is to be in the power of strong drink. We know what an awful thing it is to be in the power of morphine, or cocaine, or some other kind of dope. Many of us know through stories, distressing and agonizing, that have been poured into our ears, what an awful thing it is to be in the power of lust. How many men

have come to me in despair this past year and told the
story of their dreadful slavery. It is an awful thing to be
in the power of sin of any kind.

There is, however, a way to get free. There is a way by
which any man or woman who is the slave of any sin of
any kind can get instantaneous and complete deliverance
from the power of that sin. There is, however, only one
way. That way is by doing the right thing with Jesus
Christ. The Apostle Paul was once in the power of sin.
He was once helplessly and hopelessly enslaved. With all
the power of an unusually strong will he tried to break
away from the power of sin, but the more he tried to
break away, the more completely he seemed to be in sin's
grip forever, until at last, in utter despair, he cried, "O
wretched man that I am! who shall deliver me out of the
body of this death?" (Rom. 7:24). And then he found
Christ and took Him as his Deliverer from the power of
sin, and he found perfect freedom and cried again, "I
thank God through Jesus Christ our Lord" (Rom. 7:25).
You cannot get out of sin's power unless you do the right
thing with Jesus Christ. You may get free from some bad
habits. You may, for example, give up drinking without
the help of Christ, though very few do; but whether you
do or do not, you will not get out of sin's grip, you will
simply turn from one sin to another. Christ alone can save
you from sin's power. I could stand here by the hour and
tell you of men and women I have personally known, men
and women as completely enslaved by sin in one form or
another as any man or woman who ever walked the earth,
whom the Lord Jesus Christ has set free when they did the
right thing with Him.

4. In the fourth place, you will get great joy by doing
the right thing with Jesus Christ. The Apostle Peter says

"On whom, though now ye see him not, yet believing, ye rejoice greatly with joy unspeakable and full of glory (I Peter 1:8). You can get "joy unspeakable and full of glory" by doing the right thing with Jesus Christ. You cannot get joy unspeakable and full of glory in any other way. You know happy people, of course, who are not Christians, but you do not know any one who is not a Christian who has "joy unspeakable and full of glory." You do not know any one who is not a Christian who has the deep, constant, satisfying, and overflowing joy, that those men and women have who are not merely nominal Christians but real Christians, those men and women who have fully accepted Christ as their personal Saviour and are really trusting God for the forgiveness of all their sins because they fully believe God's testimony concerning Jesus Christ having borne every one of their sins when He died on the cross, thus fully settling their sins forever, and who have without reservation surrendered the entire control of their thoughts and lives to Jesus Christ, and who are confessing Jesus Christ as their Lord before the world every reasonable opportunity they get, and who are watching for every opportunity to lead others to Christ, and who are serving Jesus Christ with all their strength every day.

Do the right thing with Jesus Christ and you get this wonderful joy. Reject Jesus Christ and you lose it. How foolish men and women are! There are many men in this audience tonight who are rejecting Christ because they think they will lose joy if they take Christ. Are you blind, men? Do you not see that those who have taken Christ really are happier than you are? Do you not see that many Christians are happier in poverty than skeptics and world-lings are in wealth? Are you deaf, women? Have you not heard many whose word you must believe, and from all ranks of society, testify that they have found a joy since they took Christ that they never dreamed of in the world?

I do not think that many of you could tell me much that I do not know about this world's joys. I have tasted pretty much all of them, but I never knew "joy unspeakable and full of glory" until I took Jesus Christ. I do now. My every day is full of joy. I have perplexities, I have annoyances, I have experiences that could easily prove exasperating. I have burdens of many kinds, I have what may appear to be great losses, I have things said to me and written to me, and said and printed about me, that would cut to the quick if I did not know the Lord Jesus; but, through all, every day is unspeakably happy. Not so long ago I had more things come to me that might have caused grief and anxiety and worry and heartache and deep sorrow than in almost any other week of my life, but it was a radiantly happy week. Why? Simply because of what Jesus Christ is to me, and what He is to me, just because I have done the right thing with Him.

5. In the fifth place, if you do the right thing with Jesus Christ you will get eternal life. Eternal Life! What a wonderful phrase that is, eternal life. Life that never ends! Life that knows no death! Life of unutterable beauty and dignity and honor and glory and rapture! Life that is endless in its duration and perfect in its quality! Life like the life of God Himself. *Eternal life!* What has the world to put in comparison with that? What is the wealth of a millionaire compared with eternal life? I would rather be a penniless pauper all my days, living in destitution and hunger and rags and cold, and have eternal life, than to roll in wealth all my days and have all that wealth can buy, and not have eternal life. I have no envy of the rich.

No, I know their lives and hearts too well. I have often a greater pity for them than for the poor, for often they are more to be pitied than the poor. The life of the average millionaire is a sad, sad life.

What is the wisdom of the world's greatest scientist or philosopher compared with eternal life? What are the honors of a great general or a mighty ruler of men compared with eternal life? What are the pleasures of the most successful votary of pleasure compared with eternal life? Put all the world has, absolutely everything the world can give, into one pan of the scales. Put eternal life into the other scale. See the world's side go up. It is lighter than the smallest dust of the balance in comparison with eternal life. *Eternal life!* Oh, who can fathom all the depth of meaning that there is in these two wondrous words?

And you get it by simply doing the right thing with Jesus Christ. Do the right thing with Jesus Christ and you get eternal life. Do the wrong thing with Jesus Christ and you lose eternal life. Listen to God's own Word about that, John 3:36, "He that believeth on the Son *hath eternal life:* and he that believeth not the Son *shall not see life;* but the wrath of God abideth on him." Listen to God's Word again, "And the witness is this, that God gave unto us eternal life, and this life is in his Son. He that hath the Son hath the life; he that hath not the Son of God hath not the life" (I John 5:11, 12).

Are you going to do the right thing with Jesus Christ now and get eternal life, or are you going to do the wrong thing with Jesus Christ and forever lose eternal life?

6. But there is something better even than eternal life that you get by doing the right thing with Jesus Christ. By doing the right thing with Jesus Christ you become a child of God, an heir of God and joint heir with Jesus

Christ. We read in God's own Word, in John 1:12, "As many as received him, to them gave he the right to become children of God, even to them that believe on his name." And in Romans 8:17 we read, "If children, then heirs; heirs of God, and joint heirs with Christ." Just think of that a moment, a child of God, and an heir of God, and a joint heir (or fellow heir) with Jesus Christ. We have heard these words very often but have we ever stopped to weigh their meaning and to take in their wondrous import? A *child of God!* Think of it! God the Infinite One, God the Creator of all things, God to whom the whole race of men and the whole company of angels is as nothing, less than a speck of dust is in comparison to the whole earth; God in comparison with whom the greatest of philosophers, the mightiest of monarchs, and the purest of saints is less than the most ignorant idiot is in comparison with the greatest philosopher—and we to become His children and His heirs! Heirs of all this Infinite God is and all this Infinite God has. It staggers the mind to try to think of it. That is what is open to each one of us. That is what is open to you and open to me by just doing the right thing with Jesus Christ.

One day, years ago, I met the son and heir of one of the richest men in the whole world, and he invited me to dinner. As I sat and talked with him it seemed to me as if it might be in some respects a fine thing to be the son and heir of the richest millionaire on earth. But that is nothing, just nothing at all, to being a child of God, an heir of God and fellow heir with Jesus Christ. That is what is open to us, to each one of us; but it can be obtained in only one way, and that is by doing the right thing with Jesus Christ. Do the right thing with Jesus Christ and in a moment you become a child of God, an heir of God and fellow heir with Jesus Christ. Listen to God's own statement about it again, "As many as received him, to them gave he the right to become children of God, even to them that believe on his name" (John 1:12).

Do the wrong thing with Jesus Christ and you lose forever your chance of becoming a child of God, an heir of God and fellow heir with Jesus Christ. Oh, what a loss that is! The loss of untold wealth, the loss of earth's greatest honors, the loss of dearest friends, is nothing in comparison with the loss of becoming a child of God, an heir of God and fellow heir with Jesus Christ. That is the awful cost of doing the wrong thing with Jesus Christ. We see, then, something of what we gain by doing the right thing with Jesus Christ, and something of what we lose by doing the wrong thing with Jesus Christ. By doing the right thing with Jesus Christ we gain forgiveness of all our sins. By doing the right thing with Jesus Christ we gain peace of conscience. By doing the right thing with Jesus Christ we gain deliverance from sin's power. By doing the right thing with Jesus Christ we gain joy unspeakable and full of glory. By doing the right thing with Jesus Christ we gain eternal life. By doing the right thing with Jesus Christ we become children of God, heirs of God, and fellow heirs with Jesus Christ. Is it not evident, then, that the most important question of this day and of all days is, "What shall I do then with Jesus, which is called Christ?"

But what will you do with Him? Will you do the right thing with Him, or will you do the wrong thing with Him? Will you do the right thing and gain all, or will you do the wrong thing and lose all? I put the question to each individual reader. What will you do with Jesus? It does not matter whether you are a church member or not, I put the question to you, What will you do with Jesus? I put the question to the most worldly man or woman here as well as to the most religious, "What will you do with Jesus who is called Christ?" I put the question to the one who is most sunken in sin, for there is hope for you of getting all these things if you do the right thing with Jesus Christ, just as much as there is for the most moral and upright and highly respected man or woman here—"What then will you do with Jesus which is called Christ?" Of each one of you I ask, Will you do the right thing with Jesus Christ, or will you do the wrong thing with Jesus Christ?

7. But there is something better than anything I have mentioned yet that depends entirely on what you do with Jesus Christ. If you do the right thing with Jesus Christ, then some day you will become just like Him. Listen to what God says, "Behold, what manner of love the Father hath bestowed upon us, that we should be called the children of God: and such we are. . . . Beloved, now are we the children of God, and it is not yet made manifest what we shall be. We know that, when he shall be manifested, *we shall be like him;* for we shall see him even as he is" (I John 3:1, 2). "What," someone will say, "can I become like Jesus Christ?" Yes, even you can become just like Jesus Christ. Think of it! You and I, with all our present failings, with all our shortcomings, meannesses and pettinesses, some of which we do not see but others see very clearly, for they stick out all over us and generally they stick out most conspicuously on those of us who have the best opinion of ourselves—even we can become just like Him, be like Him in every perfection and glory of His matchless, faultless, glorious, Divine character. Yes, and we can be like Him in the glory of His outward ap-

pearance too; for it is written in the Word of God, "For our citizenship is in heaven; from whence also we wait for a Saviour, the Lord Jesus Christ: who shall fashion anew the body of our humiliation, that it may be conformed to the body of his glory, according to the working whereby he is able even to subject all things unto himself" (Phil. 3:20, 21). And how can we become just like Him? By doing the right thing with Jesus Christ.

II. What Is the Right Thing to Do with Jesus Christ?

1. First of all, the right thing to do with Jesus Christ is to receive Him, to receive Him as your Saviour. This is evident from the verse that we have quoted already a number of times, John 1:12, "As many as received him, to them gave he the right to become children of God, even to them that believe on his name." He died for your sins. "All we like sheep have gone astray; we have turned every one to his own way; and Jehovah hath made to strike on him the iniquity of us all" (Is. 53:6). Will you accept Him as your sin-bearer? Will you say, "Oh, God, I believe what Thy Word says about Jesus Christ. I believe He bore my sins in His own body on the cross. I believe every one of my sins was laid on Him and settled fully and forever when He died on the cross in my place. And I now take Him as my sin-bearer. Forgive all my sins for Jesus Christ's sake"?

Take Him not only as your Saviour from the guilt of sin but also as your Saviour from the power of sin. He not only died to make atonement for your sins, He also rose again, and He lives today to set you free from the power of sin and to make intercession for you (Heb. 7:25). Will you take Him now as your Deliverer from the power of sin? Will you come to this risen and mighty Lord Jesus with all your weakness and sins and trust Him to set you free? That is the right thing to do with Jesus Christ: just take Him as your Saviour, your crucified Saviour, from the guilt of sin and your risen Saviour from the power of sin.

2. The next right thing to do with Jesus is to let Him into your heart. He says, "Behold, I stand at the door, and knock: if any man hear my voice, and open the door, I will come in to him, and will sup with him, and he with me" (Rev. 3:20). Jesus is standing at the door of every heart. He is knocking at the door of every heart. Will you open the door and let Him in? Who will? Who will say, "Lord Jesus, come in; come in and reign"?

3. The next right thing to do with Jesus is to enthrone Him in your heart. He is the Christ, God's anointed King, because God has made Him so. As Peter said on the day of Pentecost, "God hath made him both Lord and Christ, this Jesus whom ye crucified" (Acts 2:36). Will you enthrone Him as King in your heart? Will you say honestly to Him, "Lord Jesus, take the throne of my heart and live and reign there supreme"? Who will do it?

4. Once more, the right thing to do with Jesus Christ is to confess Him before the world as your Lord and Master. He Himself says in Matthew 10:32, 33, "Every one therefore who shall confess me before men, him will I also confess before my Father which is in heaven. But whosoever shall deny me before men, him will I also deny before my Father which is in heaven." And Paul says in Romans 10:9, 10, "If thou shalt confess with thy mouth Jesus as Lord, and shalt believe in thy heart that God raised him from the dead, thou shalt be saved: for with the heart man believeth unto righteousness; and with the

mouth confession is made unto salvation." Who will do it?

There is just one more right thing to do with Jesus. What is it? Go tell others about Him, when you yourself have taken Him as your Saviour and let Him into your heart, and enthroned Him as King and confessed Him before the world as your Lord.

When Jesus was here on earth He cast several thousand demons out of a wretched man who was in their control. The condition of that man before he met Jesus was awful beyond description, but the condition of that man after he met Jesus was glorious beyond description. And that man naturally wanted to go with Jesus wherever He went. But Jesus said, "No, do not go away with me, but stay right here and go to your home, and declare how great things God hath done for thee. And he went his way publishing throughout the whole city how great things Jesus had done for him" (Luke 8:38, 39).

Oh, if you have taken Jesus go tell every one you can about Him and bring every one you can to Him.

These are the right things to do with Jesus. Who will do them now and gain all that is worth having for time and for eternity? Who of you will take Him as your Saviour? Who of you will listen to His voice and let Him into your heart? Who of you will enthrone Him in your heart as King? Who of you will begin the confession of Him as your Lord?

IX. How God Guides

Nevertheless I am continually with thee: thou hast holden my right hand. Thou shalt guide me with thy counsel, and afterward receive me to glory.

PSALM 73:23, 24.

THERE ARE no promises of God's Word more precious to the man who wishes to do His will, and who realizes the goodness of His will, than the promises of God's guidance. What a cheering, gladdening, inspiring thought is that contained in the text, that we may have the guidance of infinite wisdom and love at every turn of life and that we have it to the end of our earthly pilgrimage.

There are few more precious words in the whole Book of Psalms, which is one of the most precious of all the books of the Bible, than these: "Thou hast holden my right hand. Thou shalt guide me with thy counsel, and afterwards receive me to glory." How the thoughtful and believing and obedient heart burns as it reads these wonderful words of the text! I wish we had time to dwell on the characteristics of God's guidance as they are set forth in so many places in the Word of God, but we must turn at once to consideration of the means God uses in guiding us.

1. God Guides by His Word

First of all, God guides by His Word. We read in Psalm 119:105, "Thy word is a lamp unto my feet, and a light unto my path," and in the 130th verse of this same Psalm we read, "The entrance of thy words giveth light; it giveth understanding unto the simple." God's own written Word is the chief instrument that God uses in our guidance. God led the children of Israel by a pillar of cloud by day and a pillar of fire by night. The written Word, the Bible, is our pillar of cloud and pillar of fire. As it leads we follow. One of the main purposes of the Bible, the Word of God, is practical guidance in the affairs of everyday life. All other leadings must be tested by the Word. Whatever promptings may come to us from any other source, whether it be by human counsel or by the prompting of some invisible spirit, or in whatever way it may come, we must test the promptings, or the guidance or the counsel, by the sure Word of God, "To the law and to the testimony; if they speak not according to this Word, it is because there is no light in them" (Is. 8:20). Whatever spirit or impulse may move us, whatever dream or vision may come to us, or whatever apparently providential opening we may have, all must be tested by the Word of God. If the impulse or leading, or prompting, or vision, or providential opening is not according to the Book, it is not of God. "The prophet that hath a dream, let him tell a dream; and he that hath my word, let him speak my word faithfully. What is the chaff to the wheat? saith the LORD" (Jer. 23:28). If Christians would only study the Word they would not be misled as they so often are by seducing spirits, or by impulses of any kind, that are not of God but of Satan or of their own deceitful hearts. How often people have said to me that the Spirit was leading them to do this or that, when the thing that they were being led to do was in direct contradiction to God's Word. For example, a man once called on me to consult me about marrying a woman who he said was a beautiful Christian, that they had deep sympathy for the work of God, and that the Spirit of God was leading them to marry one another. "But," I said to the man, "you already have one wife." "Yes," he replied, "but you know we have not gotten on well together." "Yes," I said, "I know that, and, furthermore, I have had a conversation with her and believe it is your fault more than hers. But, however that may be, if you should put her away and marry this other woman, Jesus Christ says that you would be an adulterer." "Oh, but," he replied, "the Spirit of God is leading us to one another." Now, whatever spirit may have been leading that man, it certainly was not the Spirit of God, for the Spirit of God cannot lead anyone to do that which is in direct contradiction to the Word of God. I replied to this man, "You are a liar and a blasphemer. How dare you attribute to the Spirit of God action that is directly contrary to the teaching of Jesus Christ?" Many, many times Christian people have promptings from various sources which they attribute to the Holy Spirit, but which are in plain and flat contradiction to the clear and definite teachings of God's Word. The truth is, many so neglect the Word that they are all in a maze regarding the impulses and leadings that come to them, as to whence they are; whereas, if they studied the Word they would at once detect the real character of these leadings.

But the Word itself must be used in a right way if we are to find the leading of God from it. We have no right to seek guidance from the Word of God by using it in any fantastic way, as some do. For example, there is no warrant whatever in the Word of God for trying to find out God's will by opening the Bible at random and putting a finger on some text without regard to its real meaning as made clear by the context. There is no warrant whatever in the Bible for any such use of it. The Bible is not a talisman, or a fortune-telling book, it is not in any sense a magic book; it is a revelation from an infinitely wise God, made in a reasonable way, to reasonable beings, and we obtain God's guidance from the Bible by taking the verse of Scripture in which the guidance is found, in the connection in which it is found in the Bible, and interpreting it, led by the Holy Spirit, in its context as found in the Bible. Many have fallen into all kinds of fanaticism by using their Bible in this irrational and fantastic way. Some years ago a prediction was made by a somewhat prominent woman Bible teacher that on a certain date Oakland and Alameda and some other California cities, and I think also Chicago, were to be swallowed up in an earthquake. The definite day was set and many were in anticipation, and many in great dread. A friend of mine living in Chicago was somewhat disturbed over the matter and sought God's guidance by opening her Bible at random, and this was the passage to which she opened:

Moreover the word of the Lord came to me saying, Son of man, eat thy bread with quaking, and drink thy water with trembling and with carefulness; and say unto the people of the land, Thus saith the Lord God of the inhabitants of Jerusalem, and of the land of Israel: They shall eat their bread with carefulness, and drink their water with astonishment, that her land may be desolate from all that is therein, because of the violence of all them that dwell therein. And the cities that are inhabited shall be laid waste, and the land shall be desolate; and ye shall know that I am the Lord. And the word of the Lord came unto me, saying, Son of man, what is that proverb that ye have in the land of Israel, saying, The days are prolonged, and every vision faileth? Tell them therefore, Thus saith the Lord God;

I will make this proverb to cease, and they shall no more use it as a proverb in Israel; but say unto them, The days are at hand, and the effect of every vision. For there shall be no more any vain vision nor flattering divination within the house of Israel. For I am the Lord: I will speak, and the word that I shall speak shall come to pass; it shall be no more prolonged: for in your days, O rebellious house will I say the word, and will perform it, saith the Lord God. Again the word of the Lord came to me, saying, Son of man, behold they of the house of Israel say, The vision that he seeth is for many days to come, and he prophesieth of the times that are far off. Therefore say unto them, Thus saith the Lord God; There shall none of my words be prolonged any more, but the word which I have spoken shall be done, saith the Lord God (Ezek. 12:17-28).

Of course, this seemed like a direct answer, and, if it were a direct answer, it clearly meant that the prophecy of the destruction of Oakland, Alameda, and Chicago would be fulfilled at once, on the day predicted. The woman told me of this that very day, but I was not at all disturbed. As we all know, the prophecy was not fulfilled, and this would-be prophetess sank out of sight, and, so far as I know, has not been heard from since. Many years afterward an earthquake did come to San Francisco and work great destruction, but San Francisco was not in this woman's prophecy, and Oakland and Alameda were, and they were left practically untouched by the earthquake, and certainly did not sink out of sight as the woman had predicted. And, furthermore, the earthquake that came to an adjoining city was many years after the prophesied date. This is only one illustration among many that might be given of how utterly misleading is any guidance that we get in this fantastic and unwarranted way.

Furthermore, the fact that some text of Scripture comes

into your mind at some time when you are trying to discover God's will is not by any means proof positive that it is just the Scripture for you at that time. The devil can suggest Scripture. He did this in tempting our Lord (Matt. 4:6), and he does it today. If the text suggested, taken in its real meaning as determined by the language used and by the context, applies to your present position, it is, of course, a message from God for you, but the mere fact that a text of Scripture comes to mind at some time, which by a distortion from its proper meaning might apply to our case, is no evidence whatever that it is the guidance of God. May I repeat once more than in getting guidance from God's Word we must take the words as they are found in their connection, and interpret them according to the proper meaning of the words used and apply them to those to whom it is evident from the context that they were intended to apply. But with this word of warning against seeking God's guidance from the Word of God in fantastic and unwarranted ways, let me repeat that God's principal way of guiding us, and the way by which all other methods must be tested, is by His written Word.

II. God Leads by His Spirit

God also leads us by His Spirit, that is, by the direct leading of the Spirit in the individual heart. Beyond question, there is such a thing as an "inner light." We read in Acts 8:29, "And the Spirit said unto Philip, Go near and join thyself to this chariot." In a similar way, we read in Acts 16:6, 7, of the Apostle Paul and his companions: "And they went through the region of Phrygia and the region of Galatia, having been forbidden of the Holy Spirit to speak the word in Asia; and when they were come over against Mysia they assayed to go into Bithynia; and the

Spirit of Jesus suffered them not." In one of these passages we see God by His Holy Spirit giving direct personal guidance to Philip as to what he should do, and in the other passage we see the Spirit restraining Paul and his companions from doing something they otherwise would have done. There is no reason why God should not lead us as directly as He led Philip and Paul in their day, and those who walk near God can testify that He does so lead. I was once walking on South Clark Street, Chicago, near the corner of Adams, a very busy corner. I had passed by hundreds of people as I walked. Suddenly I met a man, a perfect stranger, and it seemed to me as if the Spirit of God said to me, "Speak to that man." I stopped a moment and stepped into a doorway and asked God to show me if the guidance was really from Him. It became instantly clear that it was. I turned round and followed the man, who had reached the corner and was crossing from one side of Clark Street to the other. I caught up to him in the middle of the street. Providentially, for a moment there was no traffic at that point. Even on that busy street we were alone in the middle of the street. I laid my hand on his shoulder as we crossed to the farther sidewalk, and said to him, "Are you a Christian?" He replied, "That is a strange thing to ask a perfect stranger on the street." I said, "I know it is, and I do not ask every man that I meet on the street that question, but I believe God told me to ask you." He stopped and hung his head. He said, "This is very strange. I am a graduate of Amherst College, but I am a perfect wreck through drink here in Chicago, and only yesterday my cousin, who is a minister in this city, was speaking to me about my soul, and for you, a perfect stranger, to put this question to me here on this busy street!" I did not succeed in bringing the man to a decision there on the street, but shortly afterward he was led to a definite acceptance of Christ. A friend of mine walking the busy streets of Toronto suddenly had a deep impression that he should go to the hospital and speak to someone there. He tried to think of someone he knew at the hospital and he could think of but one man. He took it for granted that he was the man he was to speak to, but when he reached the hospital and came to this man's bedside there was no reason why he should speak to him, and nothing came of the conversation. He was in great perplexity, and standing by his friend's bed he asked God to guide him. He saw a man lying on the bed right across the aisle. This man was a stranger, he had been brought to the hospital for an apparently minor trouble, some difficulty with his knee. His case did not seem at all urgent, but my friend turned and spoke to him and had the joy of leading him to Christ. To everybody's surprise, that man passed into eternity that very night. It was then or never. So God often guides us today (if we are near Him and listening for His guidance), leading us to do things that otherwise we would not do, and restraining us from doing things we otherwise would do. But these inward leadings must be always tested by the Word, and we do well when any prompting comes to look up to God and ask Him to make clear to us if this leading is of Him, otherwise we may be led to do things which are absurd and not at all according to the will of God.

But though it is oftentimes our privilege to be thus led by the Spirit of God, there is no warrant whatever in the Word of God for our refusing to act until we are thus led. Remember, this is not God's only method of guidance. Oftentimes we do not need this particular kind of guidance. Take the cases of Philip and of Paul to which we have referred. God did not guide Philip and Paul in this way in every step they took. Philip had done many things in coming down through Samaria to the desert where he met the treasurer of Queen Candace, and it was not until the chariot of the treasurer appeared that God led Philip directly by His Spirit. And so with Paul, who in the missionary work to which God had called him had followed his own best judgment as God enlightened it until the moment came when he needed the special direct prohibition of the Holy Spirit of his going into a place where God would not have him go at that time. There is no need for our having the Spirit's direction to do that which the Spirit has already told us to do in the Word. For example, many a man who has fanatical and unscriptural notions about the guidance of the Holy Spirit refuses to work in an after-meeting because, as he says, the Holy Spirit does not lead him to speak to anyone, and he is waiting until the Holy Spirit does. But as the Word of God plainly teaches him to be a fisher of men (Matt. 4:19; 28:19; Acts 8:4), if he is to obey God's word, whenever there is opportunity to work with men he should go to work, and there is no need of the Holy Spirit's special guidance. Paul would have gone into these places to preach the Gospel if the Holy Spirit had not forbidden him. He would not have waited for some direct command of the Spirit to preach, and when we have an opportunity to speak to lost souls we should speak, unless restrained. What we need is not some direct impulse of the Holy Spirit to make us speak, the Word already commands us to do that; what we need, if we are not to speak, is that the Spirit should directly forbid us to speak.

Furthermore, let me repeat again that we should bear in mind about the Spirit's guidance, that He will not lead us to do anything that is contrary to the Word of God. The Word of God is the Holy Spirit's book, and He never contradicts His own teaching. Many people do things that are strictly forbidden in the Word of God, and justify themselves in so doing by saying the Spirit of God guides them to do it; but any spirit that guides us to do something that is contrary to the Holy Spirit's own book cannot by any possibility be the Holy Spirit. For example, some time ago, in reasoning with one of the leaders of the Tongues Movement about the utterly unscriptural character of their assemblies, I called his attention to the fact that in the 14th chapter of 1st Corinthians we have God's explicit command that not more than two, or, at the most, three, persons should be allowed to speak "in a tongue" in any one meeting, and that the two or three that did speak must not speak at the same time, but "in turn," and if there were no interpreter present, not even one should be allowed to speak in a tongue, that (while he might speak in private with himself in a tongue, even with no interpreter present) he must "keep silence in the church." I called this man's attention to the fact that in their assembly they disobeyed every one of these three things that God commanded. He defended himself and his companions by saying, "But we are led by the Spirit of God to do these things, and therefore are not subject to the Word." I called his attention to the fact that the Word of God in this passage was given by the Holy Spirit for the specific purpose of guiding the assembly in its conduct and that any spirit that led them to disobey these explicit commandments of the Holy Spirit Himself, given through His Apostle Paul and recorded in His Word, could not by any possibility be the Holy Spirit. Here, again, we should always bear in mind that there are spirits other than the

Holy Spirit, and we should "try the spirits whether they be of God," and we should try them by the Word. One of the gravest mistakes that anyone can make in his Christian life is that of being so anxious for spirit guidance that he is willing to open his soul to any spirit who may come along and try to lead him.

Further still, we should always bear in mind that there is absolutely no warrant in the Word of God for supposing that the Holy Spirit leads into strange and absurd ways, or does strange and absurd things. For example, some have certain signs by which they discern, as they say, the Holy Spirit's guidance. For example, some look for a peculiar twitching of the face, or for some other physical impulse. With some the test is a shudder, or cold sensation down the back. When this comes they take it as clear evidence that the Holy Spirit is present. In a former day, and to a certain extent today, some judge the Spirit's presence by what they call "the jerks," that is, a peculiar jerking that takes possession of a person, which they suppose to be the work of the Holy Spirit. All this is absolutely unwarranted by the Word of God and dishonoring to the Holy Spirit. We are told distinctly and emphatically in II Timothy 1:7 that the Holy Spirit is a spirit "of power, and of love, and of a sound mind." The word translated "sound mind" really means "sound sense," and, therefore, any spirit that leads us to do ridiculous things, cannot be the Holy Spirit. There are some who defend the most outrageous improprieties and even indecencies in public assemblies, saying that the Holy Spirit prompts them to these things. By this claim they fly directly in the face of God's own Word, which teaches us specifically in I Corinthians 14:32, 33 "The spirits of the prophets are subject to the prophets; for God is not a God of confusion, but of peace." And in the 40th verse we are told that "all things" in a Spirit-governed assembly should be "done decently and in order." The word translated "decently" in this passage means "in a becoming [or respectable] way," which certainly does not permit the disorders and immodesties, and confusions and indecencies and absurdities that occur in many assemblies that claim to be Spirit led, but which, tested by the Word of God, certainly are not led by the Holy Spirit.

III. God Guides Us by Enlightening Our Judgment

In the third place, God guides us by enlightening our judgment. We see an illustration of this in the case of the Apostle Paul in Acts 16:10. God had been guiding Paul by a direct impression produced in his heart by the Holy Spirit, keeping him from going to certain places whither otherwise he would have gone. Then God gives to Paul in the night a vision, and, having received the vision, Paul, by his own enlightened judgment, concludes from it what God has called him to do. This is God's ordinary method of guidance when His Word does not specifically tell us what to do. We go to God for wisdom, we make sure that our wills are completely surrendered to Him, and that we realize our dependence on Him for guidance, then God clears up our judgment and makes it clear to us what we should do. Here again we should always bear in mind that "God is light and in him is no darkness at all," and that, therefore, God's guidance is clear guidance, and we should not act until things are made perfectly plain. Many miss God's guidance by doing things too soon. Had they waited until God had enabled them to see clearly, under the illumination of His Holy Spirit, they would have avoided disastrous mistakes. The principle that "he that believeth shall not make haste" (Is. 28:16) applies right here. On the other hand, when any duty is made clear we should do it at once. If we hesitate to act when the way is made clear, then we soon get into doubt and perplexity and are all at sea as to what God would have us do. Many and many a man has seen the path of duty as clear as day before him, and, instead of stepping out at once, has hesitated even when the will of God has become perfectly clear, and before long was plunged into absolute uncertainty as to what God would have him do.

IV. God May Guide by Visions and Dreams

In Acts 16:9, 10, we are told how God guided Paul by a vision, and there are other instances of such guidance, not only before Pentecost, but after. God may so guide people today. However, that was not God's usual method of guiding men, even in Bible times, and it is even less His usual way since the giving of His Word and the giving of the Holy Spirit. We do not need that mode of guidance as the Old Testament saints needed it, for we now have the complete Word and we also have the Spirit in a sense and in a fullness that the Old Testament saints did not have. God does lead by dreams today. When I was a boy, sleeping in a room in our old home in Geneva, N. Y., I dreamed I was sleeping in that room and that my mother, who I dreamed was dead (though she was really living at the time) came and stood by my bed, with a face like an angel's, and besought me to enter the ministry, and in my sleep I promised her that I would. In a few moments I awoke and found it all a dream, but I never could get away from that promise. I never had rest in my soul until I did give up my plans for life and promise God that I would preach. But the matter of dreams is one in which we should exercise the utmost care, and we should be very careful and prayerful and Scriptural in deciding that any dream is from God. Only the other day a brilliant and highly educated woman called at my office to tell me some wonderful dreams that she had and what these dreams proved. Her interpretation of the dreams was most extraordinary and fantastic. But while dreams are a very uncertain method of guidance, it will not do for us to say that God never so guides, but it is the height of folly to seek God's guidance in that way, and especially to dictate that God shall guide in that way.

V. God Does Not Guide by Casting Lots in This Dispensation

In Acts 1:24-26 we learn that the apostles sought guidance in choosing by lot one to take the place of Judas. This method of finding God's will was common in the Old Testament times, but it belongs entirely to the old dispensation. This is the last case on record. It was never used after Pentecost. We need today no such crude way of ascertaining the will of God, as we have the Word and the Spirit at our disposal. Neither should we seek signs. That belongs to the imperfect dispensation that is past, and even then it was a sign of unbelief.

VI. God Guides by His Providence

God has still another way of guiding us besides those already mentioned, and that is by His providences, that is, He so shapes the events of our lives that it becomes clear that he would have us go in a certain direction or do a certain thing. For example, God puts an unsaved man directly in our way so that we are alone with him and thus have an opportunity for conversation with him. In such a case we need no vision to tell us, and we need no mighty impulse of the Holy Spirit to tell us, that we ought to speak to this man about his soul. The very fact that we are alone with him and have an opportunity for conversation is of itself all the Divine guidance we need. We do need, however, to look to God to tell us what to say to him and how to say it, but God will not tell us by some supernatural revelation what to say, but by making clear to our own minds what we should say.

In a similar way, if a man needs work to support himself or family, and a position for honest employment opens to him, he needs no inner voice, no direct leading of the Holy Spirit, to tell him to take the work; the opening opportunity is of itself God's guidance by God's providence.

We must, however, be very careful and very prayerful in interpreting "the leadings of providence." What some people call "the leading of providence" means no more than the easiest way. When Jonah was fleeing from God and went down to Joppa he found a ship just ready to start for Tarshish (Jonah 1:3). If he had been like many today he would have interpreted that as meaning it was God's will that he should go to Tarshish, as there was a ship just starting for Tarshish, instead of to Nineveh, to which city God had bidden him go. In point of fact, Jonah did take ship to Tarshish but he was under no illusion in the matter, he knew perfectly well that he was not going where God wanted him to go, and he got into trouble for it. Oftentimes people seek guidance by providence by asking God to shut up a certain way that is opening to them, if it is not His will that they should go that way. There is no warrant whatever for doing that. God has given us our judgment and is ready to illuminate our judgment, and we have no right to act the part of children and to ask

Him to shut up the way so we cannot possibly go that way if it is not His will. Some fancy that the easy way is necessarily God's way, but oftentimes the hard way is God's way. Our Lord Himself said, as recorded in Matthew 16:24, "If any man would come after me, let him deny himself, and take up his cross and follow me." That certainly is not the easy way. There are many who advise us to "follow the path of least resistance," but the path of least resistance is not always God's way by any means.

Some ask God to guide them providentially by removing all difficulties from the path in which He would have them go, but we have no right to offer such a prayer. God wishes us to be men and women of character and to surmount difficulties, and oftentimes He will allow difficulties to pile up in the very way in which we ought to go, and the fact that we see that a path is full of difficulties is no reason for deciding it is not the way God would have us go. Nevertheless, God does guide us by His providence, and we have no right to despise His providential guidance. For example, one may desire to go to China or to Africa as a missionary, and God does not give him the health requisite for going to China or to Africa. He should take that as clear providential guidance that he ought not to go, and seek some other opportunity for serving God.

Many people are asking God to open some door of opportunity, and God does open a door of opportunity right at hand, but it is not the kind of work they would especially like to do, so they decline to see in it a door of opportunity. The whole difficulty is that they are not wholly surrendered to the will of God.

Before we close this subject let us repeat again what cannot be emphasized too much or too often, that all leadings, whether they be by the Spirit, by visions, by providences, by our own judgment, or by advice of friends, or in any other way, must be tested by the Word of God.

The main point in the whole matter of guidance is absolute surrender of the will to God, delighting in His will, and willingness to do joyfully the very things we would not like to do naturally, the very things in connection with which there may be many disagreeable circumstances, because, for example, of association with, or even subordination to, those that we do not altogether like, or difficulties of other kinds. It is to do joyfully what we are to do, simply because it is the will of God, and the willingness to let God lead in any way He pleases, whether it be by His Word, or His Spirit, or by the enlightening of our judgment, or by His providence, or by whatever way He will. If only we will completely distrust our own judgment and have absolute confidence in God's judgment and God's willingness to guide us, and are absolutely surrendered to His will, whatever it may be, and are willing to let God choose His way of guidance, and will go on step by step as He does guide us, and if we are daily studying His Word to know His will, and are listening for the still small voice of the Spirit, going step by step as He leads, He will guide us with His eye; He will guide us with His counsel to the end of our earthly pilgrimage, and afterward receive us into glory.

X. God's Keeping

OUR SUBJECT is God's keeping and how to make sure of it. How to enjoy or make sure of God's keeping will come out when we reach a consideration of whom God keeps. The Bible, both the Old and New Testaments, is full of passages on this important subject of God's keeping, and we shall look at quite a number of them, but no one of them can properly be considered the text of the entire sermon. I am going to give you a Bible reading rather than a sermon. Let us look first at John 17:11, which comes nearer being the text of the whole sermon than any other, "And I am no more in the world, and these are in the world, and I come to thee. Holy Father, keep them in the name which thou hast given me, that they may be one even as we are." This was Jesus' prayer. I am glad He offered it; for the Father heareth Him always, and I am sure of God's keeping because the Lord Jesus asked that I might be kept. Most wonderfully does this prayer of our Lord and Saviour bring out the security of those who belong to Him. In the next verse He goes on to say that while He was with His disciples He kept them in the Father's name. Yes, He says more than that, He says, "I guarded them, and not one of them perished." The son of perdition perished, and he was one of the apostolic company, but he was never really one of those who belonged to Christ, he was not one of those whom the Father had given to Jesus

Christ. Christ Himself declares that Judas was a devil from the beginning (John 6:70). But now our Lord was leaving His disciples, and He turned their keeping over to the Father, and it is now the Father who keeps us, and it is this keeping which we are now to study. What the Bible tells us of God's keeping can be classified under five main heads: (1) Whom God keeps; (2) What He keeps; (3) From what He keeps; (4) How He keeps; (5) Unto what He keeps.

I. Whom God Keeps

We look first at whom God keeps, by discovering which we will find out how any one of us may be sure of His glorious keeping.

1. Whom He keeps we are told in the very verse that we have just been reading, John 17:11, 12. Here the Lord Jesus prays to the Father to keep those whom the Father Himself hath given to Christ, and says that He himself during His earthly life had kept those whom His Father had given Him. Those whom God keeps, then, are those who belong to Christ, those whom the Father has given to Him. The clear teaching of these verses is that there is a body of persons who belonged in a peculiar way to God, and whom God gave to His Son. This company of people, and their security and privileges, are frequently mentioned in the Gospel of John. Those whom God keeps are those who belong to this company. The way then to be sure of God's keeping is to make sure that we belong to this company whom the Father has given to Christ. But who are these, and how can any one of us tell whether or not we belong to this privileged company?

(1) This question is answered in John 6:37, in which Jesus is recorded as saying, "All that which the Father giv-

eth me shall come unto me; and him that cometh to me I will in no wise cast out." From this it is clear that all those who come to Christ belong to that elect company whom the Father has given to Him. Every man who really comes to Christ, comes to Him as his Saviour, as his Master, as his Lord, and commits himself unreservedly to Him, for Christ to save and to rule. He is one of those whom God has given to Christ, and whom God therefore keeps. Are you one of this number? Have you come to Christ in this real way? If you are, God will keep you. If not, will you come to Christ today and thus make sure that you will be kept?

(2) We have still another description of those whom God has given to Christ. In John 17:6, He says, "I manifested thy name unto the men whom thou gavest me out of the world: thine they were and thou gavest them to me; and they have kept thy word." Here we are told that those whom the Father gave to the Son were those who kept God's Word. Everyone who keeps God's Word may be sure that he belongs to the elect company whom God the Father Himself will keep. Notice carefully Christ's description of them: "They have kept thy word." That is to say, they not only hear God's Word, not only obey it—they keep God's Word, that is, they treasure it, they regard it as their most precious treasure, and they will not give it up for any gain that may be offered them in place of it. These are those whom God keeps. If we keep God's Word, God Himself will keep us. Are you keeping God's Word?

2. Isaiah 26:3, also tells us whom God keeps. Here the prophet says, in speaking to God, "Thou wilt keep him in perfect peace, whose mind is stayed on thee: because he trusteth in thee." God keeps the one whose mind is

stayed on Him, the one who looks not at self but at God, looks not at circumstances but at God; the one who puts confidence in God. The "keeping" of this passage is different from that which is spoken of in John 17. There it is a keeping from perishing, here it is a keeping from all anxiety and worry. We shall see this more clearly when we come to speak of what God keeps us from.

II. What God Keeps

Now let us look at what God keeps. Paul tells us in II Timothy 1:12 just what God keeps. He says, "I know whom I have believed, and am persuaded that he is able to keep [guard] that which I have committed unto him against that day." The word translated "keep" in this passage in the Revised Version is rendered "guard," but it is the same word that is used in John 17:2, though not the same word that is used in John 17:11. Here we are taught that God keeps (or guards) that which is committed unto Him. Some commit more unto God, some less, but what is committed unto Him He keeps. Some commit the keeping of their souls unto God (I Pet. 4:19), some commit their temporal affairs to Him, some commit their health to Him, some more, some less, but whatever is committed to Him He keeps. Dorothea Trudel, a German woman, tells how her mother was a woman of great faith in prayer, and though her father was a drinking man, who made little or no provision for the family, and the children numbered eleven, and their straits were sometimes great, they always were saved from suffering. She says: "There were times when we had not a farthing left in the house. None but God knew of our condition, and He who feedeth the young ravens when they cry was not unmindful of the petitions of His faithful child. He ever helped us in our time of need. It was on this account that our mother's favorite motto, 'Pray, but do not beg,' was so impressed on our minds. When one of the children was asked on what her mother relied in her poverty, the child said, 'On God alone.' She never tells us how God is going to help, but she is always certain His aid will come at the right time." The experience of this German woman could be duplicated in the experience of thousands in our own land and other lands. It was related of Mrs. Jane C. Pithey, a member of the Centenary Methodist Church in Chicago, that for years she was disabled by the shaking palsy and received all her supplies in answer to prayer. When her husband died he left in his pocketbook two silver quarters. Besides the little cottage, this was all that she had to support herself and a bedridden mother of nearly ninety years of age. It is said "she went to God in prayer and day by day each want was met. Each needed article was asked for by name until her hired girl was astounded at the constant answers given. One morning as Mrs. Pithey was rising from her knees at the family worship, the girl burst out, 'You have forgotten to pray for coal and we are entirely out.' So, as she stood, she added a petition for the coal. About an hour after, the bell rang; she went to the door, and there was a load of coal sent by a man who knew nothing of her want, and who had never sent anything before, nor ever has since." Many other instances are related of God's keeping and supplying all her needs. Some commit their work to God, some commit everything. His keeping will be just in proportion to our committing.

III. From What God Keeps

1. First of all, God keeps those who belong to His Son Jesus Christ from perishing. This comes out very plainly

in the passage with which we started, John 17:11, 12. Our Lord prayed, "Holy Father, keep them in thy name, which thou hast given me, that they may be one even as we are." Then He goes on to say, "While I was with them, I kept them in thy name which thou hast given me: and I guarded them, and not one of them perished, but the son of perdition." The one who truly comes to Christ, the one who enters with his whole heart in the fellowship of Christ, the one who fully receives Christ as his Saviour from the guilt and power of sin, the one who wholeheartedly and unreservedly surrenders to Christ as his Master, him God keeps from ever perishing. No matter how numerous, how subtle, how mighty the assaults of Satan, of sin, and of error may be, God will keep him. As the Lord Jesus puts it in another place (John 10:28, 29), "I give unto them eternal life; and they shall never perish, and no one shall snatch them out of my hand. My Father which hath given them unto me, is greater than all and no one is able to snatch them out of the Father's hand." This is the position of the one who belongs to Christ, the almighty hand of Jesus Christ the Son underneath him, the almighty hand of God the Father over him, and there he is, in between those two almighty hands, perfectly sheltered, and no person and no power in heaven or earth or hell can ever get him.

2. But it is not only from perishing that God keeps; He also keeps from falling. As we read in Jude 24, He "is able to keep us from falling and to present us faultless before the presence of his glory with exceeding joy." The word translated "falling" in this passage is translated "stumbling" in the Revised Version, and this is the exact force of the word. One may fall without perishing, but one need not even fall, indeed he need not even stumble. God can

keep us from even this, and will keep us from this if we look to Him and trust Him to do it. But when we get our eyes off Him down we go, but He still keeps us from perishing. He sees to it that we get up again, even if we do stumble. Though we stumble, we are still kept, just as Peter was, from making utter shipwreck. Peter was in Satan's sieve, but, nevertheless, he was still kept by God in answer to Christ's intercessory prayer, and Christ always lives to make intercession for us and so "is able to save to the uttermost" (Heb. 7:25). What comfort there is in this verse to him who hesitates to begin the Christian life because he knows his weakness and is afraid that he will stumble and fall. If only you will put yourself wholly in God's hands He is able, no matter how weak you may be in yourself, to keep you even from stumbling.

3. But it is not only from perishing and from stumbling that God keeps, He keeps the one whose mind is stayed on Him in perfect peace. This glad gospel we find in that book in the Old Testament which is so full of the Gospel, the prophecy of Isaiah. We read in Isaiah 26:3, "Thou wilt keep him in perfect peace, whose mind is stayed on thee: because he trusteth in thee." Then Isaiah goes on to say, "Trust ye in the Lord forever: for in the Lord Jehovah is everlasting strength." God keeps from all anxiety those who may stay their minds on Him. If only we will take our eyes off ourselves and off men, and off circumstances, and stay our minds on God, and on Him alone and on His sure promises, He will keep us in perfect peace. These are precious words for such a time as that in which we live, where one does not know any morning when he takes up his paper what he may read. No matter how perilous our position may seem, no matter how unlooked for and how unwelcome our surroundings may be, if we stay our minds

on the Lord Jehovah He will keep us in perfect peace. We have an illustration of this in Caleb and Joshua in the Old Testament (Num. 13:17, 26, 28, 29, 30; 14:1, 3, 7-9). The ten spies that accompanied Caleb and Joshua into the land looked at circumstances and were filled with dismay. Caleb and Joshua looked away from circumstances, they looked right over the heads of the giants, they looked at God and His Word. They stayed their minds on Him and He kept them in perfect peace. It was so with Paul also in the awful storm and impending shipwreck in the Mediterranean. The crew and soldiers were cowering with fear as they heard the howling of the wind and saw the fierceness and force of the dashing waves, but Paul looked over the waves and over the storm at God and His Word, and stayed His mind on Him, and God kept Him in perfect peace so that Paul could say to his cowering companions, "Sirs, be of good cheer: for I believe God that it shall be even so as it has been spoken unto me" (Acts 27:25). Oh, we need men and women of just such imperturbable calm as that in such days of stress and storm as those in which we are now living. If only we would stay our minds on God, if only we would really trust Him, if only we would really believe His Word, that it will be even as it has been told us, we would never have a single ruffle of anxiety. There is one passage in the Word of God which, taken alone, would be able, if only we would bear it in mind and believe it, to banish all fears and all anxiety forever. That passage is Romans 8:28, "We know that all things work together for good to them that love God, to them who are the called according to his purpose." Whatever comes to us must be one of the "all things," and if we believed this passage we would know that however threatening it may appear, and however bad in itself it may really be, it must work together for our highest good with the other things that God sends into our lives. How, then, can we ever have a moment's worry?

IV. How God Keeps

1. We are told in Deuteronomy 32:9, 10, that Jehovah keeps His People "as the apple of his eye." The eye is the most wonderfully protected portion of the body, and "the apple," or pupil, of the eye is the most important part of the eye, the lens, and is especially provided for and protected. The mechanism of the eye and the provision for its welfare that God has made has always awakened the wonder and admiration of men of science. It is shielded and guarded in every conceivable way, and just so, with every conceivable and inconceivable safeguard, God protects His people from injury. Every year brings into view some new provision God has made for our safety.

2. We are taught in Genesis 28:15, that God keeps those who trust and obey Him "in all places whithersoever" they go. He kept Joseph in his father's house; He kept Joseph in the pit in the wilderness; He kept Joseph in Potiphar's house; He kept Joseph in the Egyptian prison; He kept Joseph in the palace. God kept David from the fury and power of the lion and the bear as he watched the sheep in the wilderness; He kept David in security through all the years that Saul hunted him like a partridge in the mountains (I Sam. 26:20); He kept David in the face of the many foes that arose against him when he became king; God kept him everywhere, so that David could write, "Yea, though I walk through the valley of the shadow of death, I will fear no evil, for thou art with me." And so God keeps us if we trust and obey Him, in all places whithersoever we go.

3. In Psalm 121:3, 4, we are taught God keeps His people at all times. He that keeps us never "slumbers nor sleeps." We are kept not only in all places, but also at all times. God is never off guard, He never sleeps at His post. Satan can never catch one of God's children when their Watchman is sleeping. I am glad of this. You and I are often off guard. Satan can often catch us napping, but he can never catch us when our Watchman is napping.

4. But there is another thought about God's keeping which, if possible, is even more precious, and that is, He keeps to all eternity. Here again we think of John 10:28, "I give unto them eternal life: and they shall never perish, and no one shall snatch them out of my hand." Those who trust in Christ shall "never perish." This is one of the most precious facts about God's keeping, it never ends. We may prove unfaithful, but He ever abideth faithful, He cannot deny Himself (II Tim. 2:13). He keepeth to the end. We shall never perish, or, to translate more literally as well as more expressively, "in no wise [shall we] perish, for ever." We stand today and look forward into the never-ending future. If we know ourselves well and look at ourselves alone we may well tremble at the thought of how utterly we may fail some time in those ever rolling years; but if we look up to God and know Him, we will not tremble, for He never faileth, and we have His Word for it that He will ever keep us. He keeps me today "as the apple of his eye," He will keep me in all places, He will keep me at all times, He will keep me to all eternity.

V. Unto What God Keeps

We have seen whom God keeps; we have seen what God keeps; we have seen from what God keeps; we have seen how God keeps; one thought remains, Unto what does God keep? This question is answered in I Peter 1:5: We "are kept by the power of God unto a salvation ready to be revealed in the last time." On this we have no time to dwell. Simply let me say this, that the salvation that we have today, no matter how complete it may seem, even though we know not only the forgiveness of sins and adoption into the family of God, but also deliverance from sin's power, a life of daily victory, is not the whole of salvation. Completed salvation lies in the eternal future. It includes not merely the salvation of the spirit and the soul, it includes the salvation of the body; that "salvation ready to be revealed in the last times" is the salvation that we shall possess when the wondrous promises about our being transformed into the perfect likeness of Jesus Christ, not only spiritually and morally and mentally, but also physically, have their fulfillment. It is unto that salvation that God keeps us.

Beloved fellow believer in God and in Jesus Christ His Son, have you realized fully what God's keeping means? Have you enjoyed the security that is yours, and the rest of mind that might be yours? Have you put as much into His hands to keep as He is willing to keep? Are you letting Him keep you in perfect peace in the midst of the trial and uncertainty and travail and turmoil and storm and stress of these trying days? If not, will you do it today?

And friends, you who are not Christians, do you not see how precious a thing God's keeping is? Is it not immeasurably better than anything this world has to give? Some trust in riches, some in their own abilities, some in powerful friends, some in national leaders and "preparedness," but better, infinitely better, is it to trust in God, for "he will keep him in perfect peace whose mind is stayed upon him, because he trusteth in him." Will you not put your trust in Him and have a share in this wondrous prayer of the Saviour, "Holy Father, keep through thine own name those whom thou hast given me"?

XI. The Secret of Abiding Peace

Enoch walked with God: and he was not; for God took him.

GENESIS 5:24.

OUR SUBJECT is "The Secret of Abiding Peace. Abounding Joy, and Abundant Victory in War Times and at All Times." You will find the text in Genesis 5:24, "Enoch walked with God: and he was not; for God took him." In the description of Enoch's walk given in our text we find the secret of abiding peace, abounding joy, and abundant victory in war times and at all times. To my mind, the text is one of the most fascinating and thrilling verses in the entire Bible. It sounds more like a song from a heavenly world than a plain statement of historical facts regarding a humble inhabitant of this world of ours, but such it is, and it is possible for each one of us so to live and act that it may be recorded of us, "He walked with God," and later, "and he was not; for God took him." The position of this verse in the Bible is significant and suggestive. There has been, in the verses immediately preceding, a very prosaic, monotonous, and, at first sight, tedious recital of how one man after another of the olden time lived so many years, begat a son, continued to live so many years, and begat sons and daughters, and then died. Then suddenly Enoch is introduced and the story begins just as the other stories

165

begin and goes on just as the other stories go on, and seems about to end just as the other stories end, but, no, there is this fresh breath from heaven and these melodious tones sound out: "And Enoch walked with God; and he was not; for God took him." Then the story goes on again in the same old strain. Remember that this account belongs to a far-away time, thousands of years before Christ, and about a thousand years before the Flood, and yet what depth of truth and beauty there is in it. Are there not lessons for us to learn from that far, far-away olden time? The entire authentic history of Enoch is contained in nine verses in the Bible, six in the Old Testament, three in the New. History outside of the Bible is utterly unacquainted with him, yet he stands out as one of the most remarkable and admirable men of whom history speaks, a man whom God honored as He has honored but one other member of the entire race. Enoch's greatness was of the kind that pleases God. We are told in the 11th chapter of Hebrews and the fifth verse that "he hath had witness borne to him that before his translation he had been well pleasing to God." Quite likely his greatness did not win very hearty commendation from his contemporaries. However, that was not of much consequence. His greatness did not consist of military renown, political power, profound scholarship, successful statesmanship, splendid artistic or architectural genius, or even of magnificent philanthropic achievement. It was greatness of a more quiet and less pretentious and visible nature, but of a far more real and lasting nature; it was greatness of character. "He walked with God," and God so enjoyed his society that He took Enoch to be with Himself permanently.

I wish to make clear to you all three things: first, what

it is to walk with God; second, what are some of the results of walking with God; third, how we may get into such a walk ourselves.

I. What Is It to Walk with God?

First of all, I think I may safely say that for some of us here this morning that question needs no answer. God Himself has answered it to us in blessed, unspeakably blessed, experience. But for others of us—yes, many of us —it does need an answer. We have read the words of the text before, perhaps we have read them often. They have charmed us, soothed us, thrilled us, and yet often the question has arisen in our hearts, Just what do they mean? This question admits of a very plain and simple answer: to walk with God means to live one's life in the consciousness of God's presence and in conscious communion with Him, to have the thought constantly before us, "God is beside me," and every now and then to be speaking to Him, and, still more, listening for Him to speak to us. In a word, to walk with God is to live in the real, constant, conscious companionship of God. We read that Enoch walked with God, not on a few rare occasions of spiritual exaltation, such perhaps as most of us have known, but for three hundred consecutive years after the birth of Methuselah (Gen. 6:22). It is possible for us to have this consciousness of the nearness and fellowship of God in our daily life, to talk with Him as we talk with an earthly friend; yes, as we talk with no earthly friend, and to have Him talk to us, and to commune with Him in a silence that is far more meaningful than any words could be. I would gladly linger here in this sweet and holy place, but let us pass on to the results of walking with God.

II. The Results of Walking with God

1. The first result of walking with God is great joy, abounding joy. "In thy presence," sings the Psalmist, "is fullness of joy" (Ps. 16:11). There is no greater joy than that which comes from right companionship. Who would not rather live in a hut with congenial companions than in a palace with disagreeable associates? Who would not rather live on a bleak and barren isle among real Christians than in the fairest land the sun ever shone upon among infidels, blasphemers, drunkards, ruffians, and libertines? The most attractive feature of heaven is its society, especially the society of God and the Lord Jesus. Well might Samuel Rutherford say: I would rather be in hell with Thee than in heaven without Thee: for if I were in hell with Thee that would be heaven to me, and if I were in heaven without Thee that would be hell to me." But when we have the conscious presence and companionship of God on earth, "we have two heavens, the heaven to which we are going and a heaven to go to heaven in." In one of the loneliest hours of His lonely life Jesus looked up with radiant joy and said, "Yet I am not alone, because the Father is with me" (John 6:32).

Can you not remember some ecstatic hour of your life when you walked, and sometimes talked and sometimes were silent, with an earthly companion whom you loved as you loved no other? Oh, happy hour! but only faintly suggestive of the rapture that comes from walking with God, for He is an infinitely dearer and better and more glorious companion than any earthly one could be. How the homely details of everyday life are transfigured if we have the constant fellowship of God in them. There lived in the Middle Ages a lad named Nicholas Hermann. He was a raw, awkward youth, breaking all things that he touched, but one day the thought was brought to his mind with great force that God was everywhere and that he might have the constant thought of God's presence with him and do all things to God's glory. This thought transformed his life. He soon went to a monastery. His duty there was of the most menial character—in the kitchen, washing pots and kettles, but, to use his own way of putting it, he "practised the presence of God" in the midst of his humble toil. That kitchen became so holy a place that men took long journeys to meet Nicholas Hermann and to converse with him. Some of his conversations and letters have been published under the title *The Practise of the Presence of God*.

2. The second result of walking with God is a great sense of security, of abiding peace. In the Psalm already quoted the Psalmist sings again: "I have set the Lord always before me, because he is at my right hand I shall not be moved" (16:7). Certainly not. How can we be moved if God is with us? What harm can befall us? How often God says to His servants as they begin to tremble before approaching danger: "Fear not, I am with thee" (Isa. 41:10). How safe the trusting child feels with father or mother by its side. A little girl was once playing in a room below while her mother was above, busy about household duties. Every little while the child would come to the foot of the stairs and call up: "Mamma, are you there?" "Yes, darling, what is it?" "Nothing, I only wanted to know if you were there." Then again a little while: "Mamma, are you there?" "Yes, darling, what is it?" "Nothing, I only wanted to know if you were there." Ah! is not that all we want to know, that God is here, right here by our side? There may be pestilence, there may be war, there may be famine, there may be thugs on the street, there may be burglars in the

house, there may be haunts of sin, and unprincipled men and women on every hand; yes, our wrestling may not be with flesh and blood but "against the principalities, against the powers, against the world rulers of this darkness, against the spiritual hosts of wickedness in the heavenlies," but what does it matter? God is with us. Oh, if only we bore in mind at every moment the thought of His presence with us, if only we could hear Him saying, "Fear thou not, for I am with thee; be not dismayed, for I am thy God: I will strengthen thee; yea I will help thee; yea I will uphold thee with the right hand of my righteousness," there would never be one single tremor of fear in our hearts under any circumstances. No matter how the war increases, no matter how near it may come to our own doors, there would be unruffled calm, abounding peace. We could constantly say, under all circumstances, "The Lord is my light and my salvation; whom shall I fear? The Lord is the strength of my life; of whom shall I be afraid? When the wicked, even my enemies and my foes came upon me to eat up my flesh, they stumbled and fell. Though a host should encamp against me, my heart shall not fear: though war should rise against me, in this will I be confident." No wonder the Psalmist wrote in this connection, "One thing have I desired of the Lord, that will I seek after; that I may dwell in the house of the Lord all the days of my life, to behold the beauty of the LORD, and to inquire in his temple." The conscious companionship of God is the great secret of abiding peace.

3. The third result of walking with God is spiritual enlightenment. Communion with God rather than scholarship opens to us the mind and thought of God. There is no hint that Enoch was a man of science or letters. I am very sure he was not a higher critic, and yet this plain man

by walking with God and talking with God got such an insight into the purposes of God as no other man of his time had. In the Epistle of Jude, the 14th and 15th verses, we learn that even in that far-away day, a thousand years before the flood, Enoch got hold of the great truth of the second coming of Christ. So today some old washerwoman, or some humble cobbler, who walks with God may know more of the mind of God than many an eminent college professor, or even a professor in a theological seminary. The important question concerning points in dispute in religion and spiritual life is not what do the scholars say, but what do the men and women who walk with God say. If one is considering going to some one for spiritual instruction, the first question is not how much of a scholar is he, not how much does he know of Latin and Hebrew and Greek and Syriac and philosophy and psychology, but does he walk with God? This is the great condition of spiritual insight, wisdom, and understanding.

4. The fourth result of walking with God is purity of heart and life. Nothing else is so cleansing as the consciousness of God's presence. Things that we have long tolerated become intolerable when we bring them into the white light of the presence of the Holy One. How many things we do in the darkness of the night, yea, even in the broad light of day, that we could not for a moment think of doing if we realized God was right there by our side— looking. Many deeds we now do would be left undone if we realized this. Many words we now speak would be left unspoken, many thoughts and fancies we now cherish would be speedily banished. There are certain things that we do in the absence of certain holy friends that we would not for a moment do in their presence, but God is always present, whether we know it or not, and if we walk in the

consciousness of His presence, if we walk with God, our lives and hearts will speedily whiten. I have a friend who in his early life, though he professed to be a Christian, was very profane. He tried hard to overcome his profanity, but failed. He felt he must give up his attempt to be a Christian, but one day a wise Christian to whom he appealed for help, said to him, "Would you swear if your father were present?" "No." "Well, when you go to your work tomorrow remember that God is with you every moment. Keep the thought of God's presence with you." At the end of the day, to his amazement, he had not sworn once. He had had the thought of God with him through the day and he could not be profane in that presence. The consciousness of the presence of God will keep us from doing all the things that we would not dream of doing in His presence. Herein lies the secret of a holy life.

5. The next result of walking with God is closely akin to this, beauty of character. We become like those with whom we habitually associate. How like their parents children become. How many mothers and fathers have been startled by seeing their own imperfections and follies mirrored in their children. Husband and wife grow strangely like one another, thus also the one who associates with God becomes like God. If we walk with God, more and more will His beauty illumine and reflect itself in our lives. Moses' very face shone as he came down from the forty days and forty nights of converse with God. So will our whole life soon shine with a heavenly glow and glory if we habitually walk with God. "With unveiled faces reflecting as a mirror the glory of God" we shall be "transformed into the same image from glory unto glory" (II Cor. 3:18).

6. The next result of walking with God will be eminent

usefulness. Our lives may be quiet and even obscure; it may be impossible to point to what men call great achievement, but the highest usefulness lies not in such things but in the silent, almost unnoticed but potent and pervasive influence of a holy life, whose light illumines, whose beauty cheers, and whose nobility elevates all who come in contact with it. Enoch has wrought out immeasurably more good for man than Nebuchadnezzar, who built the marvelous structures of Babylon, than Augustus who "found Rome brick and left it marble," than the Egyptian monarchs who built the pyramids to amaze and mystify the world for thousands of years to come; and today the man or woman, no matter how humble or obscure, who walks with God is accomplishing more for God and man than Morse with his telegraph, Fulton with his steamboat, Stevenson with his locomotive, Cyrus Field with his Atlantic cable, Roebling with his marvelous bridges, Marconi with his wireless telegraphy and telephony, Edison and Tesla with their electric and electrifying discoveries, or any of the renowned political reformers of the day, with all their futile schemes for turning this world into a terrestrial paradise. Friends, if you wish to be really, permanently, eternally useful, walk with God.

7. But there is a still better result than this from walking with God—we please God. Before his translation Enoch had this testimony borne to him, that he "was well pleasing to God" (Heb. 11:5, R.V.). This is more than to be useful. God wants our company, God wants us to walk with Him, and He is well pleased when we do. God is more concerned that we walk with Him than that we work for Him. Martha was taken up with her service for her Lord, but Mary was taken up with her Lord Himself, and He testified that Mary had chosen the better part. It is quite

possible today to be so occupied with our work for God that we forget Him for whom we work. If we would please Him we should first see to it that we walk with him.

8. There is one result of walking with God still left to be mentioned, that is, God's eternal companionship. "Enoch walked with God: and he was not; for God took him." The man who walks on earth with God, God will sooner or later take to be with Himself forever. "If any man serve me," says Christ, "let him follow me; and where I am there shall also my servant be." If we do not walk with God on earth we are not likely to live with God in heaven. If we do not care to cultivate His society now, we may be sure that He will not take us to be in His society forever.

III. How to Enter into a Walk with God

These eight immeasurably precious results come from walking with God: abounding joy, abiding peace, spiritual enlightenment, purity of heart and life, beauty of character, eminent usefulness, pleasing God, God's eternal companionship. Do we not all then long to walk with Him? To come then face to face with the great practical question, what must we do that we ourselves may enter into this joyous, blessed walk with Him? The question can be plainly and simply answered.

1. First of all, we must trust in the atoning blood of Christ. "By faith," the record reads, "Enoch was translated" (Heb. 11:5; cf. v. 4). Comparing this with what is said immediately before about Abel, we see that the faith by which he pleased God and was translated was faith in what God said about the blood. God is holy and we are sinners. Sin separates, as a deep and impassable chasm between us and Him. There can be no walk with Him until

sin is put away and the chasm thus bridged, and it is the blood, and the blood alone, that puts away sin (Heb. 9:22). It is vain for us to attempt to cultivate the presence of God until we have accepted the provision that God Himself has made for putting away sin from between us and Himself. Indeed, if we have any real thought of God's holiness and our sinfulness there could be no joy, but only agony, in fellowship with Him, unless our sin was covered up, washed away, blotted out by the blood. There are many today who are spurning the blood and still attempting to walk with God. Vain attempt! It is utterly impossible.

2. If we would walk with God we must obey God. Jesus said, "If a man love me, he will keep my word: and my Father will love him, and we will come unto him, and make our abode with him" (John 14:23, R.V.). Obedience to God, absolute surrender to His will, is necessary if we are to walk with Him. We cannot walk with God unless we go His way. Two cannot walk together unless they be agreed (Amos 3:3). There are many who once knew the presence of God every day and every hour. They know it no longer. The old and heavenly joy has faded from their lives. They wonder why it is. Ah! there is no mystery— disobedience. Come back, get right with God, surrender anew absolutely to His will.

There is but one thing more to say. If we would walk with God we must cultivate the thought of His presence. As Nicholas Hermann, or Brother Lawrence, put it, we must "practise the presence of God" constantly. Call to mind the fact that God is with you when you are about your work. Often say to yourself, "God is with me." When you lie down at night say, "God is with me." If you wake at night remember "God is here with me." So in all the relations and experiences of life. There are four great aids to this: first, the study of God's Word. When we open this Book we realize, or ought to realize, that God Himself is speaking to us. Second, prayer. In prayer we come face to face with God. Third, thanksgiving. In intelligent and specific thanksgiving to God He is more real to us than even in petition. Fourth, worship. In worship we bow before God and contemplate Him. Oh, how near He gets at such a time. It is the Holy Spirit who will make our walk with God true and real. It is in connection with the coming of the Spirit that Christ speaks of His own manifestation of Himself to us and of the coming of the Father and of Himself to be with us (John 14:16, 17, 18, 21, 23). Look, then, to God Himself by His Spirit to make His presence known and felt.

Brethren, shall we walk with God? God is saying to each of us today, "Come, take a walk with me." If we accept the wondrous invitation He will lead us on as long as we will let Him, and some day it will be true of us, as some one has quaintly said of Enoch, we will walk so far with God that we will not come back, and so shall we ever be with the Lord.

XII. How to Be Unspeakably Happy

*Whom, not having seen ye love; on whom, though now
ye see him not, yet believing, ye rejoice greatly with joy
unspeakable and full of glory.*

I PETER 1:8.

I HAVE HERE a beautiful text, a text that you all know,
but I wonder how many of you have ever pondered it
enough to take in all its wonderful wealth of meaning.

A young woman in England many years ago always
wore a golden locket that she would not allow anyone to
open or look into, and everyone thought there must be
some romance connected with that locket and that in that
locket must be the picture of the one she loved. The young
woman died at an early age, and after her death the locket
was opened, everyone wondering whose face he would
find within. And in the locket was found simply a little
slip of paper with these words written upon it, "Whom
having not seen, I love." Her Lord Jesus was the only lover
she knew and the only lover she longed for, and she had
gone to be with Him, the one object of her whole heart's
devotion, the unseen but beloved Saviour.

But it is to the last part of the verse that I wish to call
your particular attention tonight, "On whom, though now
ye see him not, yet believing, ye rejoice greatly with joy
unspeakable and full of glory."

177

This text informs us (and many of us do not need to be informed of it, for we know it by blessed experience) that one who really believes on Jesus Christ, our unseen, but ever living Lord and Saviour, rejoices with "joy unspeakable and full of glory." The Greek word translated "joy" is a very strong word, describing extreme joy or exultant joy. The word "unspeakable" declares that this exultant joy is of such a character that we cannot, by any possibility, tell it all out to others. Everyone who really believes on the Lord Jesus does rejoice with an exultant joy that is beyond all description. And those who do truly believe on the Lord Jesus Christ are the only ones who do thus rejoice. Others may have a certain amount of joy, a certain measure of gladness, but the only people who really know "joy unspeakable and full of glory" are those who really believe on Jesus Christ.

Who is there among us who does not wish to be happy? Happiness is the one thing all men are seeking. One man seeks it in one way, and another man seeks it in another way, but all men are in pursuit of it. Even the man who is "happy only when he is miserable" is seeking happiness in this strange way of cultivating a delightful melancholy by always looking on the dark side of things. One man seeks money because he thinks that money will make a man happy. Another man seeks worldly pleasure because he thinks that worldly pleasure will make a man happy. Still another seeks learning, the knowledge of science, or philosophy, or history, or literature, because he thinks that learning brings the true joy; but they are all in pursuit of the one thing, happiness.

The vast majority of men who seek happiness do not find it. You may say what you please, but for the majority of men this is an unhappy world. I go down into the houses of the poor, I do not find many happy people there. I go into the homes of the rich, I do not find many happy people even there. Study the faces of the people you meet on the cars, on the street, at entertainments, or anywhere else, how many really radiant faces do you see? When you do see one it is so exceptional that you note it at once. But there is a way, and a very simple way, a very sure way, and a way that is open to all, not only to find happiness, but to be unspeakably happy. Our text tells us what that way is. Listen, "Oh whom, though now ye see him not, yet believing, ye rejoice greatly with joy unspeakable and full of glory." This statement of Peter's is true. How do I know it is true? In the first place, I know it is true because the Word of God says so. Whatever this book says is true. In the second place, I know it is true because I have put the matter to the test of personal experiment, and found it true. A good many people say, "I do not believe the Bible." Well, I do. I believe the Bible for a good many sufficient reasons; but there is this one reason why I believe the Bible that I wish to mention tonight: I believe the Bible because I have personally tested scores and scores of its most astonishing and apparently most incredible statements and found every one of them true in my own experience. Do you not think if I knew a man who made very many statements that I could test for myself, some of them apparently incredible, and I tested these statements one after another through a long period of years, and found every one of them true, and never one single statement failed, do you not think that I would believe that man after a while? Well, that is just my experience with the Bible, and I believe it. I would be a fool if I did not. The statement of the text is one of those that I have tested, and I have found it true.

I was not always happy. Indeed, I was once unspeakably miserable. I had sought happiness very earnestly. I had sought happiness in gaiety and sin, and found, not joy, but wretchedness. In my pursuit of happiness I had tried study, the study of languages, science, philosophy and literature, but I did not find happiness in these things. At last I turned to Jesus Christ and believed on Him, and I found not merely happiness, but something better, joy, "joy unspeakable and full of glory." Whatever heaven may be or may not be, I know that on this earth he who really believes on Jesus Christ, who puts himself in Christ's hands, to be led, and taught, and guided, and strengthened, puts himself in the hands of Jesus Christ for Jesus Christ to do all He will with him, I know that such a person finds "joy unspeakable and full of glory."

I. Why Those Who Believe in Jesus Christ Have Joy Unspeakable and Full of Glory

1. First of all, those who believe on Jesus Christ have "joy unspeakable and full of glory" because they know that their sins are all forgiven. It is a wonderful thing to know that your sins are all forgiven, to know that there is not one single, slightest cloud between you and God, to know that no matter how many, or how great your sins may have been, that they are all blotted out; to know that God has put them all behind His back, where no one can ever get at them; to know that God has sunk all your sins in the depths of the sea, from which they can never be raised; that they are all gone. A little boy once asked his mother, "Mother, where are our sins after they are blotted out?" His mother replied, "My boy, where are those figures that were on your slate yesterday?" He answered, "I rubbed them out." Then she asked, "Where are they

now?" He replied, "They are nowhere." "Well," she said, "that is just so with your sins when God has blotted them out. They are nowhere. They have ceased to be." Oh, friends, what a joy it is to know that there is not one single smallest cloud between you and the Holy God whom we call Father and who rules this universe. Suppose that you had offended against the laws of the nation and had been committed to prison on a life sentence, and a pardon were brought you, do you not think you would be happy? But that is nothing compared with the joy of knowing that your every sin is blotted out. Some years ago Governor Stuart of Pennsylvania determined to pardon one of the prisoners in the Pennsylvania State's prison, so he sent for Mr. Moody and said to him, "I have determined to pardon one of the prisoners in our state's prison, and I want you to go and take the pardon to him. You can preach to the prisoners if you want to while you are doing it." So Mr. Moody went, carrying the pardon with him, and before he began to preach he said, "I have a pardon for one of you men that the Governor has sent by me." He did not intend to tell who it was who was pardoned until the sermon was over, but as he looked around on his audience and saw how anxious they all were, how eager they were, how a very agony of suspense was in their faces, Mr. Moody thought, "This will never do, I can't keep these men in this suspense," so he said, "I will tell you now who the man is," and he read his name from the pardon. Do you not think that that was a glad moment for that one man out of those hundreds of prisoners, a glad moment for the one man who had the Governor's pardon, and who could walk out of prison a free man? Ah, but that is nothing to knowing that the eternal God has eternally pardoned your sins. Every true Christian knows that, he knows that every one of his sins is forgiven. How does he know it? Because the Bible says so in many places. For example, it says in Acts 13:39, "By him everyone that believeth is justified from all things," so we know it because God says so. But no one but the believer on Jesus Christ knows that his sins are all forgiven. If anyone who is not a believer on Jesus Christ says, "I know my sins are all forgiven," he says what is not true; for he does not know it, and cannot know it, for it is not a fact; but a Christian knows it because the Word of God says so.

The Christian knows his sins are all forgiven for another reason, that is, because the Holy Spirit bears witness in his own heart to the fact. One day, when the Apostle Peter was preaching to Cornelius, the Roman officer, and to his household, he said, "To him bear all the prophets witness that through his name everyone that believeth on him shall receive remission of sins" (Acts 10:43), and everyone in his audience believed it. The Spirit of God descended right then and there and filled their hearts with the knowledge of sins forgiven, and they "began to magnify God" with exultant hearts and exultant voices. I tell you that was a joyful meeting.

A king, a great king, once wrote one of the greatest songs that ever was written. That song has lasted through the ages. It has been sung and is still being sung by thousands. It has been sung by millions, and though it was written many centuries ago, it is just as sweet today as the day the king wrote it. The man who wrote this song was a great king, the greatest king of his day, he was also one of the greatest generals of his day, one of the greatest generals of any day. He had great armies, the all-conquering armies of the day. He had a magnificent palace. I do not suppose that any other earthly king was ever so beloved as he was. His song was about joy and about happiness. He does not say in that song, "How happy is the man who is a great king," or, "How happy is the man who is a great general." What does he say? "Oh, the happinesses of the man whose transgression is forgiven, whose sin is covered" (Ps. 32:1, translated literally from the Hebrew). There is no happiness like the joy of knowing your sins are all forgiven. Oh, what a joy thrills the heart when a man knows that his sins are fully, freely, and forever forgiven. That is one reason why he who believes on Jesus Christ is unspeakably happy, and you can have that unspeakable happiness today. I do not care how black your life may have been in the past; I do not care how far you may have wandered from God; I do not care how old you may have grown in sin; if you take Jesus Christ today for your Saviour and your Lord, and believe on Him, your every sin will be blotted out, and it will be your privilege to know it.

2. In the second place, those who believe on Jesus Christ rejoice with "joy unspeakable and full of glory" because they are free from the most grinding and crushing of all forms of slavery, the slavery of sin. There is many a slave in this audience tonight. Some of you are slaves of strong drink. Some of you men and some of you women are slaves of drink. You know you are slaves of drink. Some of you are slaves of drugs. Some of you are slaves of an ungovernable temper. Some of you are slaves of impurity of act or impurity of thought. Some of you are slaves of other sins. The grossest, vilest, most degrading slavery in the universe is the slavery of sin. Yes, many of you here tonight are slaves. But the Lord Jesus says in John 8:31, 32, "If ye continue in my word, then are ye truly my disciples; and ye shall know the truth, and the truth shall make

you free." He says again in the thirty-sixth verse, "If therefore the Son shall make you free, ye shall be free indeed." There is not a slave in this building tonight who cannot have his fetters snapped in a moment, yes, in a moment, by the mighty Son of God, if only he will believe on Jesus and trust Him to do it. How many a man and how many a woman I have known who once were slaves of sin in its most degrading and hopeless forms, who now are free.

One of the dearest and most honored and most useful friends I ever had was Sam Hadley of New York City. Sam Hadley was once hopelessly enslaved by sin. Strong drink had utterly mastered him and undermined his character. He had committed 138 forgeries, and was being sought for by the police. One night, after having spent the night before in a New York jail with delirium tremens, in a mission meeting a few blocks away from the jail he cried to Jesus to save him, and Jesus saved him right then and there; and I have often heard him say that never from that night had he ever had the slightest desire for that which had enslaved him more than anything else, intoxicating drink. My, what a happy man he became! All who knew him testified that he had "joy unspeakable and full of glory." I wish you could have looked in Sam Hadley's face and seen the joy in that redeemed and radiant countenance. But we do not need to call Sam Hadley back from heaven to testify, for there are hundreds of people right here in this building tonight who once were complete slaves, who now are God's free men and free women, and who could testify to the fact. That is one reason why we are unspeakably happy, because we are free. How the Southern Negroes rejoiced when they came to understand they were emancipated. They shouted and sang, "Glory! Glory! Hallelujah!" Why? Because once they were slaves, but now were free. No wonder, then, that we rejoice with "joy unspeakable and full of glory" because we know that we are free, and free forever.

3. In the third place, those who believe on Jesus Christ rejoice with "joy unspeakable and full of glory," because they are delivered from all fear. There is nothing that more darkens the human heart and robs it of all joy and fills it with gloom than fear in some of its myriad forms. Those who truly believe on Jesus Christ are saved from all fear. They are delivered from all fear of misfortune; they are delivered from all fear of man; they are delivered from all fear of death; they are delivered from all fear of eternity. Do you know, friends, that to a true believer in Jesus Christ "eternity" is one of the sweetest words in the English language? Oh, how it makes our hearts swell, that word, "eternity." But "eternity" is not a sweet word to the unsaved. Write these words, "Where will you spend eternity?" on a card and hand it to a man who is not a Christian, and they will make him mad; write these same words, "Where will you spend eternity?" on a card and hand it to a Christian, and they will make him glad. Why is it? Simply because a true believer on Jesus Christ is not afraid of but delights in thoughts of eternity. Why, to him who believes on Jesus Christ eternity is glory.

4. In the fourth place, he who believes on Jesus Christ rejoices with "joy unspeakable and full of glory" because he knows he will live forever. Is not that something to rejoice over? Is it not wonderful? We read in I John 2:17, "The world passeth away, and the lust thereof: but he that doeth the will of God abideth for ever." We all know that it is true that "the world passeth away." We certainly ought to know it by this time; but it is equally true that "he that doeth the will of God abideth for ever." Some-

times as we ride along our beautiful roads we see the stately mansions of our multimillionaires, and one will think, "It must be very pleasant to live there." Well, I suppose it must be, but think a moment. How long will these people live there? Perhaps the father of the household may live there ten years, possibly twenty years. Then where does he live? Some of the children may live there twenty, thirty, possibly, forty years, then what? The grave. I tell you it is not worth much after all. But the Christian looks on, and on, and on, to a life that has no end, to a life that is eternal. Glory!

5. In the fifth place, those who truly believe on Jesus Christ "rejoice greatly with joy unspeakable and full of glory" because they know they are children of God. It is a great thing to know that you are a child of God. How does the Christian know it? He knows it because God says so in John 1:12, "As many as received him, to them gave he the right to become children of God, even to them that believe on his name." A child of God, think of it! Sometimes as I have traveled around the world someone would point out to me some man, and say, "That man is the son of such and such a man, naming some king. Would you not like to be the son of a great king? Just look at that young man. He is the son of a king." In one country many years ago, when the king business was better than it is today, I was taken up and introduced to the son of one of the reigning monarchs of Europe, and the man who introduced me whispered to me, "He is the son of So-and-So" (naming the king). Well, what of it? He was a fine man in himself, but what if he was the son of a king? I am a son of God, and that is far greater, and every believer in Jesus Christ in this building tonight is a child of God, the child of "the King of kings." And any one of you here tonight, if you

are not already a child of God, can become one in an instant by receiving the Lord Jesus.

6. In the sixth place, and very closely connected with the last, true believers in Jesus Christ rejoice with "joy unspeakable and full of glory" because they are heirs of God, and joint-heirs with Jesus Christ. Is that not wonderful? We are so familiar with it we do not stop to take in the meaning of it. One of England's dukes lay dying. He called his brother to him, the one who would succeed to the title, and said, "Brother, in a few hours now you will be a duke and—and I will be a king." He was already a child of the King and in a few hours he himself would be a king. I, too, will be a king in a few days. You may say, "It may be many years." Well, many years are only a few days on the scale of eternity. And, if you really are a believer in Christ Jesus, if you have a real living faith in Him, you, too, will be a king in a few days. There was never a royal pageant sweeping through the streets of London at any coronation comparable in glory to the glory that awaits you and me just over yonder. "When Christ, who is our life, shall be manifested, then shall we also with him be manifested in glory" (Col. 3:3). We may be poor today. That does not matter. This life will be over in a moment and the other life begun, and that life is eternal.

7. In the seventh place, those who truly believe on Jesus Christ, those who throw their hearts wide open to Him, those who surrender absolutely to Him, rejoice with "joy unspeakable and full of glory" because God gives them the Holy Spirit, and there is no other joy in the present life like the joy of the Holy Spirit. One Monday morning, in Chicago, my front doorbell rang. I kept Monday in those days for my rest day, and had a notice above the doorbell, "Mr. Torrey does not see anyone on Monday." The maid

went to the door, and there stood a poor woman. The maid said, "Mr. Torrey does not see anyone on Monday. Did you not see the notice over the doorbell?" She said, "I knew that, but I have got to see him and you just go and tell him a member of his church must see him." So the maid brought her into the reception room. She was a washerwoman. The maid showed the washerwoman a seat and came upstairs and said to me, "There is a woman downstairs who is a member of your church and says she has got to see you." So down I went. As I entered the room she arose and hurried toward me, and said, "Mr. Torrey, I knew you did not see anybody on Monday, but I had to see you. Last night after I went to bed I was filled with the Holy Spirit right there in my bed, and I was so happy I could not sleep all night, and this morning I had to come and tell somebody. I could not afford to give up a day's work to come around and tell you about it, but I knew I must tell somebody and I did not know anybody I would so like to tell as you. I know you won't be angry." Indeed, I was not angry. I was glad she had come, and rejoiced with her, that old washerwoman filled with the Holy Spirit and so full of joy that, poor as she was, she had to give up a day's work to go and tell somebody she loved all about it.

Before I came to believe on the Lord Jesus Christ I was one of the bluest men who ever lived. I would sit down by the hour and brood. I have never known what the blues mean since the day I really became a Christian, absolutely surrendered to God. I have had troubles. I have had losses. There have been times in my life when I have lost pretty much everything the world holds dear. I know what it is to have a wife and four children, and to lose everything of a financial kind I had in the world, and not know from meal to meal where the next meal was coming from. I was absolutely without resources, living from hand to mouth —from God's hand to my mouth. I have known what it is to be with a wife and child in a foreign country where they spoke a strange language, and for some reason or other supplies did not come, and I did not know anyone in the city well enough to turn to for help; but I did not worry. I knew it was all in God's hands, that it would all come out right somehow, and of course it did come out right. The first time I ever visited London, thirty-nine years ago last September, I was planning to spend two weeks in England, and then start for America. I expected to find money waiting for me when I reached London, and I reached London with a wife and child, and not a letter, and no money. But I said, "The letter and the money will come tomorrow or the next day." My wife made some purchases, taking it for granted we would have money when the purchases came home; but the money did not come. Day after day passed, and the dresses came home and it was about time for the landlady to come with her board bill. It came to be the very last day before our boat started, and not a penny in sight. I went down to the bank. I did not know a soul in London. There were three or four million people there then—a stranger amid three or four millions of people, money absolutely gone, three thousand miles from friends. I did not worry. I knew the money would come. I did not know how it would come, for the source I expected to receive it from seemed utterly cut off; but yet I was happy. Why? Because I was a child of God; I had the promises of the Bible; I knew they were absolutely certain. I never lost an hour's sleep. I never worried. I just trusted. It seemed as though I would have to be fed somewhat as Elijah was, but I knew I would be fed. I knew my wife and child would be provided for. The money came, and I sailed on the steamer I expected to sail on, with every penny due paid, and money in my pocket. Friends, a Christian is happy at all times and under all circumstances. We rejoice with "joy unspeakable and full of glory" every one of the twenty-four hours of the day that we are awake, and sometimes in our sleep. You, too, can have that joy.

II. How to Get This Joy That Is Unspeakable and Full of Glory

Now arises the question, "What must anyone here tonight who has not this "joy unspeakable and full of glory" do to get it? I have really answered that question several times in what I have already said, but to be sure that we all really understand it, let me answer it again, or rather let my text answer it, "On whom, though now ye see him not, yet believing, ye rejoice greatly with joy unspeakable and full of glory." The text tells us that the way to obtain this "joy unspeakable and full of glory," the way to be unspeakably happy at all times and under all circumstances, is just by believing on the unseen Christ Jesus. What does it mean to believe on Jesus Christ? There is no mystery at all about that. It simply means to put confidence in Jesus Christ to be what He claims to be and what He offers Himself to be to us, to put confidence in Him as the One who died in our place, the One who bore our sins in His own body on the cross, and to trust God to forgive us all our sins because Jesus Christ died in our place; to put confidence in Him as the One who was raised from the dead and who now has "all power in heaven and on earth," and therefore is able to keep us day by day, and give us victory over sin, and to trust this risen Christ to give us victory over sin day by day; and to put confidence in Him as our absolute Lord and Master, and therefore to surrender our thoughts and wills and lives entirely to His control, believing everything He says, even though every scholar on earth denies it, obeying everything He commands, whatever it may cost; and to put confidence in Him as our Divine Lord, and confess Him as Lord before the world, and worship and adore Him. It is wonderful the joy that comes to him who thus believes on Jesus Christ. But one must really believe on Jesus Christ to have this joy.

Merely being a member of a church is not enough. Merely being baptized is not enough. Merely being confirmed is not enough. Merely reading your Bible is not enough. Merely reading the Prayer Book is not enough. Merely going to church is not enough. Merely going to the Lord's table and partaking of the Lord's Supper is not enough. But if you are a real believer on Jesus Christ, if you have put all your trust in the Lord Jesus as your atoning Saviour and your risen Saviour, and your risen Lord and Master, and surrendered your thoughts and life to Him utterly as your Lord and Master, and are confessing Him as such before the world, if you have thrown your heart's door wide open for the Lord Jesus to come in, and live, and rule, and reign there, you will have "joy unspeakable and full of glory" at all times and under all circumstances.

All anyone has to do, then, to be unspeakably happy at all times and under all circumstances, is to believe on Jesus Christ. It does not make any difference what his circumstances may be: he may be rich or he may be poor; he may be highly educated, or he may be ignorant; he may be in good health or he may be a hopeless invalid; he may have been a moral, clean, upright man, or he may have been the vilest of sinners, it matters not. Everyone who believes on the unseen but living Christ will find "joy unspeakable and full of glory." I can bring scores, hundreds, thousands of witnesses to prove that. You cannot bring a single witness on the other side. Col. Robert Ingersoll delighted to say, "It does not make one happy to be a Christian." How did he know? He never tried it. You can search the earth through and you cannot find me one single man or woman who was ever an out-and-out believer in Jesus Christ, a real wholehearted believer in Jesus Christ, one who had surrendered all to Jesus Christ; I say you cannot find me even one such man or woman who will deny that Jesus Christ gives "joy unspeakable and full of glory" to those who thus believe on Him. Here, then, is the way the case stands: Every single competent witness, that is, every witness who has ever tried it, testifies that believing on Jesus Christ does bring "joy unspeakable and full of glory," and these witnesses number thousands, tens of thousands and hundreds of thousands, people from every rank of society and culture, and not one witness on the other side. Is it demonstrated or not? It certainly is.

I take it that I am speaking tonight to reasonable men and women. You desire "joy unspeakable and full of glory." I have told you how to get it. There can be no doubt about it. The evidence is overwhelmingly convincing. There is, then, but one rational thing for you to do, believe on Jesus Christ tonight. Will you do it?

Once a man who was utterly miserable came to me. He was a rarely gifted man, a brilliant scholar, but utterly miserable. If ever I saw a man in hell he was the man. He had attempted suicide at least four times. He had been so near succeeding in his attempts that on two occasions it had been necessary to pump out of him the poison he had taken and thus bring him back to life. I urged him to believe on Jesus Christ. He replied, "I cannot, I have sinned away the Day of Grace." Day after day I talked with the man and always I had but one message, and that was, "Come to Jesus Christ. Believe on Jesus Christ." At last, one day the man did come to Jesus Christ. He found "joy unspeakable and full of glory." Sometimes I have seen that man when his face was radiant. Out of hell into heaven by just believing on Jesus Christ! Will you take that same step now?

XIII. The Day of Golden Opportunity

The Holy Ghost saith, Today.
HEBREWS 3:7.

THE DAY of golden opportunity is today. Golden opportunities, opportunities of priceless worth, are open to every one of us today. But "tomorrow" has no sure promise for any one of us. "The Holy Ghost saith, Today," and Conscience also cries, "Today," and the voice of Reason and the voice of History and the voice of Experience unite in one loud chorus and shout, "Today." Only the voices of lassitude and laziness and folly murmur, "Tomorrow." The Holy Ghost is ever calling, "Today." Men in their folly are forever saying, "Tomorrow."

When the frightful plague of frogs came on Pharaoh of old and on his people, Pharaoh, in his terror, sent for Moses and Aaron and said, "Entreat Jehovah, that he take away the frogs from me, and my people, and I will let the people go, that they may sacrifice unto Jehovah" (Ex. 8:8). Moses replied, "Against what time shall I entreat for thee, and for thy servants, and for thy people, that the frogs be destroyed from thee and thy houses and remain in the river only?" One would naturally suppose Pharaoh would have answered, "At once," but Pharaoh, like many another king, played the fool and answered, "Tomorrow"

194

(Ex. 8:9, 10). Men show a similar folly and often a greater folly in these days. When urged to forsake sin with its miseries and degradation and perils and turn to Christ with the joy and peace, and ennobling of our character and security that He gives, they answer, "Yes, I think I will." "When?" "Oh, tomorrow." But "the Holy Ghost saith, Today."

A poor wretch came into my office one day. He had been drinking, and drinking had brought misery into his heart and ruin into his life. I asked, "Will you quit drinking and turn to Jesus Christ?" "Oh," he exclaimed, "there is nothing else that I can do, I will." "Will you do it now?" He hung his head, and murmured, "Not now, tomorrow." But "the Holy Ghost saith, Today." Tomorrow is the devil's day and the fool's day. Today is God's day, and the wise man's day.

I wish to give you tonight some conclusive and unanswerable reasons why every man and woman in this auditorium who makes any pretensions to intelligence and common sense should not only accept the Lord Jesus as his Lord and Saviour, but should accept Him here before he leaves this building tonight, if he has not already done it. What I want to get is action, immediate action, intelligent and wise action. And the only action that is intelligent and wise for anyone who has not already accepted Jesus Christ is to accept Him right here tonight. Resolutions to do the right thing and the wise thing at some indefinite time in the future are of no value whatever. God's time is now. "The Holy Ghost saith, Today."

I. Because the Lord Jesus Brings Peace to the Tormenting Conscience

1. The first reason why every man and woman in this auditorium who has not already accepted Jesus Christ

should not only accept Him but accept Him now is because the Lord Jesus brings peace to the tormenting conscience as soon as He is accepted, and the really wise man will not only desire that peace but desire it just as soon as he can get it. Wherever there is sin there will be an accusing conscience. And we "all have sinned." If any man has sinned and his conscience does not accuse him and torment him he has sunk very low, very low. There are, of course, different degrees of torment of conscience and different kinds of torment of conscience. With some the pain is sharp and piercing, with some it is dull and grinding, but there is pain, there is unrest, there is no peace in the heart where sin has entered until that sin has been forgiven. But Jesus Christ gives peace to the most agonized conscience. Men and women have come to me in all degrees of misery over the memory of some sin they have committed, and I have pointed them to the Lord Jesus, and everyone who has really gone to Him has found rest. I could not tell how many men and women have come to me who were driven to the very verge of hopeless despair by the accusations of their conscience and were contemplating self-destruction in the hope of thus getting away from their mental agony. But I led them to Jesus Christ, and now they have rest and the peace of God that passeth all understanding.

A young man came to me one Sunday morning in Chicago in awful agony. He had sinned grievously and was reaping the harvest. He was contemplating all sorts of mad expedients to escape the inevitable consequences of his sin. I pointed him to the Son of God and the young man accepted Him. Afterward he brought to me his companion in sin. She was fully determined on a desperate deed that was likely to land her in prison or in the cemetery. I pleaded with her and pointed her to the real cure, to the Saviour. When she left me she was still undecided as to what she would do. She afterward decided and decided right. One night a long time afterward, as I was going down the back stairs of the Moody Church to the inquiry room, a young, happy-faced woman stopped me and said, "I want to thank you for what you did for me, and for my husband and for my child." I did not recognize her for a moment, and she said, "I am the young woman who came to you," and she explained the circumstances. It was the woman who had contemplated the destruction of her child, and her own destruction for time and for eternity. But she had found peace in Jesus Christ. Men and women with tormenting consciences, and with uneasy, restless hearts, there is rest for you in Jesus Christ. If you are wise you will not only find it, but you will find it now. "The Holy Ghost saith, Today." You need not spend even one more day or one more hour in the agony of your accusing, tormenting conscience.

II. Because Jesus Christ Brings Joy Unspeakable and Full of Glory to Those Who Accept Him

The second reason why every man and woman who have not already accepted Jesus Christ should not only accept Him but accept Him now is because Jesus Christ brings joy unspeakable and full of glory, a joy to which the joy of this world is as nothing in comparison, to all as soon as they really accept and confess Him. Any really wise man will not only desire this joy but desire it at once. I for one not only wish the best I can get, but I wish it as quickly as I can get it. The joy that is in Jesus Christ is the very best joy one can get. There is not a particle of doubt about that. Ask anyone who has ever tried the world and has then really tried Jesus Christ. You cannot find one single man or woman who has really tried the joy that there is in Christ, anyone who has really put his trust in Him as his personal Saviour and unreservedly surrendered to Him as his Lord and Master, who will not tell you that the world has no joy for a moment comparable with that joy which is found in Jesus Christ. No matter how rare their opportunities may have been for enjoying the world, they will tell you without the slightest hesitation that the joy that one finds in Christ is incomparably greater and finer and more satisfying than any joy the world can give. There are millions of witnesses to this fact, and their testimony is absolutely unanimous. I know the joy that comes from wealth, I know the joy that comes from the theater, I know the joy that comes from the dance, from the card table, and the joy that comes from the race course, and the joy that comes from the wine supper, and so on down to the end of the catalogue of this world's joys. I know also the joy that comes from literature and from art, the joy that comes from music, from science, from philosophy and from travel. I know practically every joy that this world has to give, but I say to you that the joy of all these put together is nothing to the joy unspeakable and full of glory that comes from a genuine acceptance of Jesus Christ as our Saviour, and a whole-hearted surrender to Him as our Lord, and a constant and open confession of Him before the world, and from receiving the Holy Spirit whom He gives to those who do thus accept Him and fully surrender to Him and confess Him. Men and women, if you wish the highest, deepest, purest, and most abounding joy, immeasurably the most satisfying joy that is to be known, not only in the life which is to come, but in the life which now is, not only come to Jesus Christ but come now. "The Holy Ghost saith, Today."

III. Because Jesus Christ Brings Deliverance from the Power of Sin

The third reason why every man and woman in this auditorium who has not already accepted Jesus Christ should not only accept Him but accept Him tonight is because Jesus Christ brings deliverance from the power of sin, and any wise man or woman not only wishes deliverance from the power of sin but wishes it as soon as he or she can get it. There is no other form of slavery known to man so degrading and so wretched as the slavery of sin. Better far be the poor black slave of the most brutal slave driver the South ever knew than to be the slave of rum, or the slave of lust, or the slave of bad temper, or the slave of dope, or the slave of an impure imagination, or the slave of greed for gold, or the slave of any other form of sin. Poor old Uncle Tom, groaning in his cabin after the cruel blows of the brutal Legree, is not so pitiable an object as yonder wretch, poor or rich, who is under the lash of appetite or of lust or of dope or of any other sin. But there is freedom right at hand, right now. Jesus Christ sets men free from sin in all its forms. He sets free men who have been slaves for years. He sets them free in a moment. Any sinner can find deliverance in Christ from any sin, can find it now. What Jesus said when He was here on earth is just as true today. "Everyone that committeth sin is the slave of sin" (John 8:34). But, thank God, it is also as true today as when He said it that, "If, therefore, the Son shall make you free, ye shall be free indeed" (John 8:36). Any man or woman who has a spark of intelligence left will not only wish deliverance from sin and its awful bondage, but wish it at once. What would you have thought of any old-time black slave of a vile and cruel master who had been offered freedom and answered, "Yes, I wish liberty. My bondage has been awful. But I don't want the freedom just yet. I will wait until next year. I will wait until next month. I will wait until next week. I will wait until tomorrow." You would exclaim, "What a fool!" But he would not be so colossal a fool as you are when you say, "Yes, I do wish deliverance from the power of sin," and then add, "but not tonight—tomorrow." Oh, men, listen, "The Holy Ghost saith, Today."

IV. Because Jesus Christ Brings Beauty of Character

The fourth reason why every man and woman who has not already accepted Jesus Christ should not only accept Him but accept Him tonight is because Jesus Christ brings beauty of character, and every wise man and woman will not only desire beauty of character, but desire it just as soon as they can get it. I sometimes notice advertisements in the papers that read, "The Secret of Beauty." I can tell you the secret of beauty, men and women, the secret of permanent, indestructible beauty. It is Jesus Christ in the heart. He not only beautifies the face, He beautifies the soul. He makes over the soul that trusts in Him into His own glorious likeness. I have seen some of the foulest men and women I ever knew made over into the fairest, and it was Jesus Christ who did it.

Sam Hadley of the Water Street Mission, New York, was the friend of all men who were down and out. He was always on the lookout for an opportunity to help some man who was about as bad as they make them onto his feet, and to lead him to Christ and to thus get the man saved. A man said to Mr. Hadley one day, "I have a friend whom I wish you would take an interest in." Sam Hadley asked, "Who is he?" "He is Bowery Ike." "Well," said Hadley, "what is he, anyhow?" The man replied, "He is a crook. He makes his living by stealing and picking pockets and all that sort of thing. Just at present he is on Blackwell's Island, serving a term there. You can find him more easily now than usual." Sam Hadley went over to Blackwell's Island and looked up Bowery Ike, and found him; for he could not get away, he was behind the bars. Bowery Ike had no use for Sam Hadley, except that when he got out he came around to Sam to get a little money to get a new suit of clothes. But he was soon off to the Island again. Every time he would come out of confinement he would go around to see Hadley, but as soon as he got on his feet again he would go back to his crooked work. Sam Hadley followed Bowery Ike for seven long years, and one day at the end of the seventh year Bowery Ike was thoroughly sick and tired of sin, and this time not only came to Sam Hadley, but came to Jesus Christ, and Jesus Christ opened His arms and took Bowery Ike in. After Bowery Ike had been saved about a year, Sam wrote me, saying, "Mr. Torrey, I have a man who wants to study at your school. They used to call him Bowery Ike. His right name is Ira Snyder. We believe in him. He has been a tough customer. He has been a hard case. But he is saved and we believe God wants to use him. Will you take him?" "Dear Sam," I replied, "I will take anybody you recommend." He wrote back, "I recommend him." Then I wrote, "Send him on." And Bowery Ike (Ira Snyder) came. Listen, men, though that man had been a crook from his boyhood, for he commenced picking pockets when a little lad; though he had been a crook nearly all his life, he became one of the most beautiful Christians I have ever met in all my life. And I say I have known thieves who have come to Christ, burglars who have come to Christ, train robbers and bank robbers who have come to Christ; I have known harlots, and murderers and people guilty of every kind of crime I ever heard of, who have come to Christ and have become some of the loveliest Christians I have ever known. Yes, some of the men and women who were once down in the deepest depths of sin. But to come back to Ira Snyder, Bowery Ike. He came on to Chicago. He stayed with us about a year, a little over a year. One night he said to me, "I want to walk home with you and have a little talk with you." On the way to my home he said, "I made a little visit down in New York a few weeks ago. I think they need me in New York. I have loved it in Chicago, I would like to stay on, but I believe they need me in New York. I have written Mr. Hadley that I am ready to go back to New York and help in the work." A few days after this Ira Snyder was taken down with influenza, a slight attack, not a very serious case, but he went to bed with it. They did not think he was very ill. But as I was leaving the dining table one night the maid told me that Mr. Hunter, who was one of my assistants there at that time, as he is now here, wished to see me. I met Mr. Hunter and he said, "Mr. Torrey, Ira Snyder is dead." I said, "What, John? You don't mean Ira Snyder?" We had another man at the Institute at the same time whose name was much the same, and who was very ill at that time, too, and I thought Mr. Hunter must mean him. "You don't mean Ira Snyder?" I said. "You must mean So-and-So," naming the other man. "No," Mr. Hunter said. "Mr. Torrey, Ira Snyder is dead. He died very suddenly." I asked, "Where is he, John?" "He is over at the undertaker's. They have prepared him for his burial and have placed him in his coffin. They are going to have the services tomorrow, and I thought I should come to tell you tonight." "That was right, John," I replied, "let us go over." We went to the undertaker's, which was not far away, and walked into the parlors. And there in a beautiful coffin lay Ira Snyder. When I looked down into that face, one of the noblest faces I have ever looked into in my life, I will tell you what I did, I could not help it, I broke down, and, leaning over, I kissed Ira Snyder's beautiful face as he lay there in his coffin. Yes, friends, Bowery Ike had been a crook before he became a Christian, but by the power of Jesus Christ in his heart he became one of the loveliest Christians I ever knew in my life. I don't think my heart ever ached over anybody outside my own family as it did over Ira Snyder, who was formerly a pickpocket, a burglar, and everything that was bad, but who in his lost and ruined condition came to Jesus, and the heart of Jesus was big enough to take him in, and Jesus came into his heart and transformed him into His own likeness. The Lord Jesus is doing that sort of thing every day.

And the Lord Jesus is also taking others who are not so foul, who, indeed, the world thinks fair, and He is making them immeasurably fairer. It is Jesus and Jesus only who makes truly lovely characters. Ah, men and women, do you not wish to be fair? Not only fair in the eyes of man, but fair in the eyes of God? You may be. It is Jesus' work to make you so. Let Him begin it at once. Let Him begin it now. "The Holy Ghost saith, Today." What do you say? "Tomorrow?" No, not if you have a particle of sense left, and I believe you have. You will say, "Tonight. Right now."

V. Because Jesus Christ Fills Our Lives with Highest Usefulness

The fifth reason why every man and woman who has not already accepted Jesus Christ should not only accept Him but accept Him now is because Jesus Christ fills our lives with highest usefulness; and every wise man and every wise woman desires not only to be useful but desires to begin being useful as soon as possible. The Christian life is the only really useful life. We look at the life of many a one who is not a Christian, and say, "There is a useful life"; but God looks at it and looks through it, looks at it in all its bearings, and writes this verdict on it, "Useless." Whether you and I see it or not, the man or woman who is not with Christ is against Him (Matt. 12:30), and the man who is against Jesus Christ is against God and against humanity. His life is useless and worse than useless. But the life that is fully surrendered to Jesus Christ becomes at once a useful life. It may be the mere wreck of a life, but it becomes at once a useful life.

A friend of mine found one of the most hopeless wrecks of womanhood in New York City and brought her to Jesus Christ. I think this poor creature lived less than two years after her conversion and many months of that time were spent on a sick bed. But that woman was used to the eternal salvation of more than a hundred persons while she lay there dying, and the story of the transformed life of "the Bluebird of Mulberry Bend" has gone around the world and saved thousands.

Come to Christ. Really come to Him. He will make you useful. Come at once, that your usefulness may begin at once. I am glad I came to the Lord Jesus when I did, but oh! if only I had come sooner. How many precious years were wasted! How many golden opportunities were lost, opportunities that will never return! Come, men and women. Come now. "The Holy Ghost saith, Today."

VI. Because the Sooner We Come to Christ, the Fuller and Richer Will Be Our Eternity

The sixth reason why every man and woman in this auditorium who has not already accepted Jesus Christ should not only accept Him but accept Him tonight is because the sooner we come to Christ, the fuller and richer will be our eternity. The eternity of each one of us will be just what we make it in the life that now is. You are constructing your eternity every day. Every day of true service for Christ makes our reward so much the greater and our eternity so much the fuller and richer. Come to Christ next Sunday and you will be behind for all eternity by as much as you might have wrought this week. You may cry in coming years, "Backward, turn backward, O Time, in thy flight," but Time will not turn backward in its flight. Time cannot turn backward. Time is flying by every moment and never returns. Today is hurrying by us at express speed. Tomorrow will soon follow. And as I turn around and peer after Yesterday and Today as they plunge into the unfathomable depths of the Past, I cry, "Yesterday, where art thou?" Out from the fathomless abyss of by-gone days comes the answer, "Gone forever." And I hear the Holy Ghost crying, "Today! Today! Today!" "The Holy Ghost saith, Today."

VII. Because If We Do Not Come to Jesus Christ Today We May Never Come At All

I will give you one more reason why every man and woman who has not already accepted Jesus Christ should not only accept Him but accept Him at once, and that is because if we do not come to Jesus Christ today we may never come at all. That is not at all a remote possibility. Thousands and tens of thousands have been as near to an acceptance of Jesus Christ as you are this moment and have said, "Not tonight," and now they have passed without Christ into that world in which there is no hope for repentance, no matter how "diligently with tears" they may seek it, into that world in which there is no opportunity to change their mind or their eternal destiny.

A man came into one of our tents one night in Chicago. It was the first time he had ever been in a meeting of that kind in his life. The words of Mr. Schiverea, who spoke that night, made a deep impression on him, and after the meeting was over he lingered with a friend and talked personally with Mr. Schiverea. His friend accepted Christ and he was on the very verge of accepting Him. Mr. Schiverea said to him, "You will accept Jesus Christ right now?" "No," the man said, "this is the first time in my life that I was ever in a meeting of this kind. I cannot decide tonight, but I promise you that I will come back Sunday night and accept Christ." It was Friday night and there was to be no meeting on Saturday. Mr. Schiverea replied that he did not question at all the honesty of the man's intention or the sincerity of his promise to return Sunday night and settle it; but added, "We have no guarantee whatever that you will live until Sunday night." "Oh," the man said, with a laugh, "you don't suppose that God is going to cut me off after the first meeting of this kind that I ever attended in my life and not give me another opportunity?" Mr. Schiverea replied, "I do not know. But I do know you are taking a great risk in waiting until Sunday night. I greatly fear that if you do not accept Jesus Christ now you will never accept Him and be lost forever." "No," the man said, "I give you my word that I will be back here Sunday night and accept Christ." Mr. Schiverea continued to plead with him, but the man would not yield. He went out of the tent with his friend. They got into a carriage and turned toward home. And as they drove up the street they passed a saloon. The man said to his friend, "Let's stop and have one more drink and then we will both swear off." "No," said his friend, "I have settled it already. I have accepted Christ and I will never take another drink." "Well," said the other, "I'm going to have one more drink, anyhow. You drive up the street and then come back for me and I will be waiting for you outside." He entered the saloon. His friend drove up the street, and after a few minutes returned to pick up the man. He was nowhere to be seen. The friend went into the saloon to look for him. He was not there. The friend went into the street again and looked up and down it for the man, but he was nowhere in sight. Passing a high board fence, he heard a groan, and passing swiftly around behind it, he discovered his friend lying behind it stabbed, with an awful gash in his body, unconscious and dying. He was taken to the Presbyterian Hospital and lived until Monday morning, but never regained consciousness and passed into eternity unsaved, lost forever. Why? Because when "the Holy Ghost said, Today," the man said, "Tomorrow." So he passed unprepared into the presence of God, and so will some of you if you do not listen to the Holy Ghost now as He saith, "Today."

One night when I was preaching in Bradford, England, a man and his wife sat side by side in the meeting and were deeply moved, but they made no decision, and gave no sign. As they walked away from the meeting the wife said to her husband, "Would it not have been nice if you and I both had risen tonight and gone forward together and both accepted Christ?" He answered, "Yes, it would." They reached home and retired. About two o'clock the following morning his wife awakened him and said, "I feel so strange." In a few minutes from that time she had passed into eternity. After he had laid his wife's body away in the cemetery, he came back to the meeting and told us this story and accepted Christ, but he came alone. Oh, men and women, listen! Do you not hear the Holy Spirit crying, "Today"?

There are so many things besides death that may make this the last opportunity you will ever have and make a refusal now final and fatal. Loss of opportunity may come. The Holy Spirit is here in power now. It is a great opportunity, the Day of Golden Opportunity. A like opportunity may never come again. It never will come again for some of you. "The Holy Ghost saith, Today."

A hardened heart may seal your doom. When a human heart is moved on by the Spirit of God, as some of your hearts are, and the heart continues to resist the Holy Spirit, it is likely to become very soon hardened and hopeless.

One night in our church in Chicago, after the meeting in which many had accepted Christ, I remained talking with a young man. He was under deep conviction, within one step of a decision. I urged on him an immediate acceptance and confession of Christ. "No," he said, "I cannot do it tonight. But I will give you my word of honor that I will come back tomorrow night and do it. I told him I did not question his word or his intention; but I said, "I have no guarantee whatever that you will keep your word. I have a feeling in my heart that if you do not settle it tonight you will never come back." "Why," he replied, "my mother is here every night. We live within a block of this place. I give you my word of honor I will come tomorrow night and settle it." Again I said, "I do not question your word, but the Spirit of God is working mightily with you tonight, and if you go out of here resisting the Spirit of God, I believe your heart will be so hardened that your eternal destiny will be sealed and you will never come back." "No," he said, "I cannot accept tonight, but I will come tomorrow night and settle it." He walked away. I watched him with a heavy heart as he passed out of the door. I said to myself, "He will never come back," and he never did. Quite a while later I asked his mother about him and she told me he had never come back into the church from that night.

Men and women, listen! You cannot trifle with God, and you cannot trifle with your own souls, and you cannot trifle with the Holy Spirit. The Holy Spirit is not only saying in our text, but He is saying in your hearts, "Today! Accept Christ right now." Will you listen to the mighty, gracious Spirit of God? Will you do as He bids you? Will you listen right now and harden not your heart, but accept Jesus Christ as your Saviour, surrender to Him as your Lord and Master, and begin to confess to Him as such before the world, and be saved, and get right here and now the wonderful blessings that He gives and that He alone can give?

XIV. Profitable Bible Study

We have considered seven profitable methods of Bible
Study. There is something, however, in Bible study more
important than the best methods, that is, the fundamental
conditions of profitable study. He who meets these condi-
tions will get more out of the Bible, while pursuing the
poorest method, than will he who does not meet them,
while pursuing the best method. Many a one who is
eagerly asking, "What method shall I pursue in my Bible
study?" needs something that goes far deeper than a new
and better method.

1. The first of the fundamental conditions of the most
profitable Bible study is that the student must be born
again. The Bible is a spiritual book, it "combines spiritual
things with spiritual words" (I Cor. 2:13, R.V. Am. Ap.),
and only a spiritual man can understand its deepest and
most characteristic and most precious teachings. "The nat-
ural man receiveth not the things of the Spirit of God: for
they are foolishness unto him; and he cannot know them,
because they are spiritually judged" (I Cor. 2:14, R.V.).
Spiritual discernment can be obtained in but one way, by
being born again. "Except a man be born anew he cannot
see the kingdom of God" (John 3:3, R.V.). No mere
knowledge of the human languages in which the Bible was
written, however extensive and accurate it may be, will
qualify one to understand and appreciate it. One must un-

210

derstand the divine language in which it was written as well, the language of the Holy Spirit. A person who understands the language of the Holy Spirit, but who does not understand a word of Greek or Hebrew or Aramaic, will get more out of the Bible than one who knows all about Greek and Hebrew and cognate languages, but is not born again, and, consequently, does not understand the language of the Holy Spirit. It is a well-demonstrated fact that many plain men and women who are entirely innocent of any knowledge of the original tongues in which the Bible was written have a knowledge of the real contents of the Bible, its actual teaching, in its depth and fullness and beauty, that surpasses that of many learned professors in theological faculties. One of the greatest follies of the day, is to get unregenerate men to teaching the Bible because of their rare knowledge of the human forms of speech in which the book was written. It would be as reasonable to set a man to teach art because he had an accurate technical knowledge of paints. It requires esthetic sense to make a man a competent teacher of art. It requires spiritual sense to make a man a competent teacher of the Bible. The man who has esthetic discernment but little or no technical knowledge of paint would be a far more competent critic of works of art than a man who has a great technical knowledge of paint but no esthetic discernment; and so the man who has no technical knowledge of Greek and Hebrew but has spiritual discernment is a far more competent critic of the Bible than he who has a rare technical knowledge of Greek and Hebrew but no spiritual discernment. It is exceedingly unfortunate that, in some quarters, more emphasis is laid on a knowledge of Greek and Hebrew in training for the ministry than is laid on spiritual life and its consequent spiritual discernment.

Unregenerate men should not be forbidden to study the Bible, for the Word of God is the instrument the Holy Spirit uses in the New Birth (I Pet. 1:23; James 1:18); but it should be distinctly understood that, while there are teachings in the Bible that the natural man can understand, and beauties which he can see, its most distinctive and characteristic teachings are beyond his grasp, and its highest beauties belong to a world in which he has no vision. The first fundamental condition of the most profitable Bible study is, then, "Ye must be born again." You cannot study the Bible to the greatest profit if you have not been born again. Its best treasures are sealed to you.

2. The second condition of the most profitable study is a love for the Bible. A man who eats with an appetite will get far more good out of his meal than one who eats from a sense of duty. It is well when a student of the Bible can say with Job, "I have treasured up the words of his mouth more than my necessary food" (Job, 23:12, R.V.), or with Jeremiah, "Thy words were found and I did eat them; and thy words were unto me a joy and the rejoicing of mine heart; for I am called by thy name, O, Lord God of hosts" (Jer. 15:16, R.V.). Many come to the table God has spread in His Word with no appetite for spiritual food, and go mincing here and there and grumbling about everything. Spiritual indigestion lies at the bottom of much modern criticism of the Bible. But how can one get a love for the Bible? First of all, by being born again. Where there is life there is likely to be appetite. A dead man never hungers. This brings us back to the first condition. But going beyond this, the more there is of vitality, the more there is of hunger. Abounding life means abounding hunger for the Word. Study of the Word stimulates love for the Word. The author can well remember the time when he

had more appetite for books about the Bible than he had for the Bible itself, but with increasing study there has come increasing love for the Book. Bearing in mind who the author of the Book is, what its purpose is, what its power is, what the riches of its contents are, will go far toward stimulating love and appetite for the Book.

3. The third condition is willingness to do hard work. Solomon has given a graphic picture of the Bible student who gets the most profit out of his study, "My son, if thou wilt receive my words, and lay up my commandments with thee; so that thou incline thine ear unto wisdom, and apply thine heart to understanding; yea, if thou cry after discernment, and lift up thy voice for understanding; if thou seek her as silver, and search for her as for hid treasures; *then* shalt thou understand the fear of the Lord and find the knowledge of God" (Prov. 2:1-5, R.V.). Now, seeking for silver and searching for hid treasures means hard work, and he who wishes to get not only the silver but the gold as well out of the Bible, and find its "hid treasures," must make up his mind to dig. It is not glancing at the Word, or reading the Word, but studying the Word, meditating on the Word, pondering the Word, that brings the richest yields. The reason why many get so little out of their Bible reading is simply because they are not willing to think. Intellectual laziness lies at the bottom of a large per cent of fruitless Bible reading. People are constantly crying for new methods of Bible study, but what many of them wish is simply some method of Bible study by which they can get all the good out of the Bible without work. If someone could tell lazy Christians some method of Bible study whereby they could put the sleepiest ten minutes of the day, just before they go to bed, into Bible study, and get the profit out of it that God intends His children shall

get out of the study of His Word, that would be just what they desire. But it can't be done. Men must be willing to work, and work hard, if they wish to dig out the treasures of infinite wisdom and knowledge and blessing which God has stored up in His Word. A business friend once asked me in a hurried call to tell him "in a word" how to study his Bible. I replied, "Think." The Psalmist pronounces that man "blessed" who "meditates in the law of the Lord day and night" (Ps. 1:2). The Lord commanded Joshua to "meditate therein day and night," and assured him that as a result of this meditation, "Then thou shalt make thy way prosperous, and then thou shalt have good success" (Josh. 1:8). Of Mary, the mother of Jesus, we read, "Mary kept all these sayings, pondering them in her heart" (Luke 2:19, R.V.). In this way alone can one study the Bible to the greatest profit. One pound of beef well chewed and digested and assimilated will give more strength than tons of beef merely glanced at; and one verse of scripture chewed and digested and assimilated will give more strength than whole chapters simply skimmed. Weigh every word you read in the Bible. Look at it. Turn it over and over. The most familiar passages get a new meaning in this way. Spend fifteen minutes on each word in Psalm 23:1, or Philippians 4:19, and see if it is not so.

4. The fourth condition is a will wholly surrendered to God. Jesus said, "If any man willeth to do his will he shall know of the teaching" (John 7:17, R.V.). A surrendered will gives that clearness of spiritual vision which is necessary to understand God's Book. Many of the difficulties and obscurities of the Bible rise wholly from the fact that the will of the student is not surrendered to the will of the author of the Book. It is remarkable how clear and simple and beautiful passages that once puzzled us become when

we are brought to that place where we say to God, "I surrender my will unconditionally to Thine. I have no will but Thine. Teach me Thy will." A surrendered will will do more to make the Bible an open book than a university education. It is simply impossible to get the largest profit out of your Bible study until you do surrender your will to God. You must be very definite about this. There are many who say, "Oh, yes, my will, I think, is surrendered to God," and yet it is not. They have never gone alone with God and said intelligently and definitely to him, "O God, I here and now give myself up to Thee, for Thee to command me, and lead me, and shape me, and send me, and do with me, absolutely as Thou wilt." Such an act is a wonderful key to unlock the treasure house of God's Word. The Bible becomes a new book when a man does that. Doing that wrought a complete transformation in the author's theology and life and ministry.

5. The fifth condition is very closely related to the fourth. The student of the Bible who would get the greatest profit out of his studies must be obedient to its teachings as soon as he sees them. It was good advice James gave to early Christians, and to us, "Be ye doers of the word, and not hearers only, deceiving your own selves." There are a good many who consider themselves Bible students who are deceiving themselves in this way today. They see what the Bible teaches, but they do not follow it, and they soon lose their power to see it. Truth obeyed leads to more truth. Truth disobeyed destroys the capacity for discovering truth. There must be not only a general surrender of the will, but specific, practical obedience to each new word of God discovered. There is no place where the law, "Unto every one that hath shall be given, and he shall have abundance; but from him that hath not shall be taken away

even that which he hath," is more gloriously certain on the one hand and more sternly inexorable on the other than in the matter of using or refusing the truth revealed in the Bible. Use, and you get more; refuse, and you lose all. Do not study the Bible for the mere gratification of intellectual curiosity, but to find out how to live and please God. Whatever duty you find commanded in the Bible, do it at once. Whatever good you see in any Bible character, imitate it immediately. Whatever mistake you note in the actions of Bible men and women, scrutinize your own life to see if you are making the same mistake, and if you find you are, correct it forthwith. James compares the Bible to a looking-glass (Jas. 1:23, 24). The chief good of a looking-glass is to show you if there is anything out of order about you; if you find there is, you can set it right. Use the Bible in that way. Obeying the truth you already see will solve the enigmas in the verses you do not yet understand. Disobeying the truth you see darkens the whole world of truth. This is the secret of much of the skepticism and error of the day. Men see the truth, but do not follow it. Then it is gone. I knew a bright and promising young minister. He made rapid advancement in the truth. He took very advanced ground on one point especially, and the storm came. One day he said to his wife, "It is very nice to believe this, but we need not speak so much about it." They began, or he, at least, to hide their testimony. The wife died and he drifted. The Bible became to him a sealed book. Faith reeled. He publicly renounced his faith in some of the fundamental truths of the Bible. He seemed to lose his grip even on the doctrine of immortality. What was the cause of it all? Truth not lived and stood for flees. Today that man is much admired and applauded by some, but daylight has given place to darkness in his soul.

6. The sixth condition is a childlike mind. God reveals His deepest truths to babes. No age needs more than our own to lay to heart the words of Jesus, "I thank thee, O Father, Lord of heaven and earth, because thou hast hid these things from the wise and prudent, and hast revealed them unto babes" (Matt. 11:25). Wherein must we be babes if God is to reveal His truth unto us, and we are to understand His Word? A child is not full of its own wisdom. It recognizes its ignorance and is ready to be taught. It does not oppose its own notions and ideas to those of its teachers. It is in that spirit we should come to the Bible if we are to get the most profit out of our study. Do not come to the Bible full of your own ideas, and seeking from it a confirmation of them. Come rather to find out what are God's ideas as He has revealed them there. Come not to find a confirmation of your own opinion, but to be taught what God may be pleased to teach. If a man comes to the Bible just to find his notions taught there, he will find them; but if he comes recognizing his own ignorance, just as a little child to be taught, he will find something infinitely better than his own notions, even the mind of God. We see why it is that many persons cannot see things which are plainly taught in the Bible. The doctrine taught is not their notion, of which they are so full that there is no room left for that which the Bible actually teaches. We have an illustration of this in the apostles themselves at one stage in their training. In Mark 9:31, we read, "He taught his disciples, and said unto them, The Son of man is delivered into the hands of men, and they shall kill him; and after that he is killed, he shall rise the third day." Now, that is as plain and definite as language can make it, but it was utterly contrary to the notions of the apostles as to what was to happen to the Christ. So we read in the next verse,

"They understood not that saying." Is not that wonderful? But is it any more wonderful than our own inability to comprehend plain statements in the Bible when they run counter to our preconceived notions? What trouble many Christians find with portions of the Sermon on the Mount that would be plain enough if we just came to Christ like a child to be taught what to believe and do, rather than coming as full-grown men who already know it all, and who must find some interpretations of Christ's words that will fit into our mature and infallible philosophy. Many a man is so full of an unbiblical theology he has been taught that it takes him a lifetime to get rid of it and understand the clear teaching of the Bible. "Oh, what can this verse mean?" many a bewildered man cries. Why, it means what it plainly says; but what you are after is not the meaning God has manifestly put into it, but the meaning you can by some ingenious trick of exegesis twist out of it and make it fit into your scheme. Don't come to the Bible to find out what you can make it mean, but to find out what God intended it to mean. Men often miss the real truth of a verse by saying, "But that can be interpreted this way." Oh, yes, so it can, but is that the way God intended it to be interpreted? We all need to pray often if we would get the most profit out of our Bible study, "Oh, God, make me a little child. Empty me of my own notions. Teach me Thine own mind. Make me ready like a little child to receive all that Thou hast to say, no matter how contrary it is to what I have thought hitherto." How the Bible opens up to one who approaches it in that way! How it closes up to the wise fool, who thinks he knows everything, and imagines he can give points to Peter and Paul, and even to Jesus Christ and to God Himself! Someone has well said the best method of Bible study is "the baby method." I was once talking with a ministerial friend about what seemed to be the clear teaching of a certain passage. "Yes," he replied, "but that doesn't agree with my philosophy." Alas! But this man was sincere, yet he did not have the childlike spirit, which is an essential condition of the most profitable Bible study. But there are many who approach the Bible in the same way. It is a great point gained in Bible study when we are brought to realize that an infinite God knows more than we, that, indeed, our highest wisdom is less than the knowledge of the most ignorant babe compared with His. But we so easily and so constantly forget this that every time we open our Bibles we would do well to get down humbly before God and say, "Father, I am but a child, teach me."

7. The seventh condition of studying the Bible to the greatest profit is that we study it as the Word of God. The Apostle Paul, in writing to the Church of the Thessalonians, thanked God without ceasing that when they received the Word of God they "accepted it not as the word of men, but as it is in truth the word of God" (I Thess. 2:13, R.V.). Well might he thank God for that, and well may we thank God when we get to the place where we receive the Word of God as the Word of God. Not that one who does not believe the Bible is the Word of God should be discouraged from studying it. Indeed, one of the best things that one who does not believe that the Bible is the Word of God can do, if he is honest, is to study it. The author of this book once doubted utterly that the Bible was the Word of God, and the firm confidence that he has today that the Bible is the Word of God has come more from the study of the Book itself than from anything else. Those who doubt it are more usually those who study about the Book, than those who dig into the actual teach-

ings of the Book itself. But while the best book of Christian evidences is the Bible, and while the most utter skeptic should be encouraged to study it, we will not get the largest measure of profit out of that study until we reach the point where we become convinced that the Bible is God's Word, and when we study it as such. There is a great difference between believing theoretically that the Bible is God's Word and studying it as God's Word. Thousands would tell you that they believe the Bible is God's Word who do not study it as God's Word. Studying the Bible as the Word of God involves four things. (1) First, it involves the unquestioning acceptance of its teachings when definitely ascertained, even when they may appear unreasonable or impossible. Reason demands that we submit our judgment and reasonings to the statements of infinite wisdom. There is nothing more irrational than rationalism, which makes the finite wisdom the test of infinite wisdom, and submits the teachings of God's omniscience to the approval of man's judgment. It is the sublimest and absurdest conceit that says, "This cannot be true, though God says it, for it does not approve itself to my reason." "Nay, but, O man, who art thou that repliest against God?" (Rom. 9:20). Real human wisdom, when it finds infinite wisdom, bows before it and says, "Speak what thou wilt and I will believe." When we have once become convinced that the Bible is God's Word its teachings must be the end of all controversy and discussion. A "thus saith the Lord" will settle every question. Yet there are many who profess to believe that the Bible is the Word of God, and if you show them what the Bible clearly teaches on some disputed point, they will shake their heads and say, "Yes, but I think so and so," or "Doctor ——, or Professor this, our church doesn't teach that way." There is little profit in that sort of Bible study. (2) Studying the Bible as the Word of God involves, in the second place, absolute reliance on all its promises in all their length and breadth. He who studies the Bible as the Word of God will not discount any one of its promises one iota. He who studies the Bible as the Word of God will say, "God, who cannot lie, has promised," and will not attempt to make God a liar by trying to make one of His promises mean less than it says. He who studies the Bible as the Word of God will be on the lookout for promises, and as soon as he finds one he will seek to ascertain just what it means, and as soon as he discovers what it means, he will step right out on that promise and risk everything on its full import. That is one of the secrets of profitable Bible study. Search for promises and appropriate them as fast as you find them, which is done by meeting the conditions and risking all on them. That is the way to make your own all the fullness of blessing God has for you. This is the key to all the treasures of God's grace. Happy is the man who has so learned to study the Bible as God's Word that he is ready to claim for himself every new promise as it appears, and to risk everything on it. (3) Studying the Bible as the Word of God involves, in the third place, obedience— prompt, exact obedience, without asking any questions to its every precept. Obedience may seem hard, it may seem impossible, but God has bidden it and I have nothing to do but to obey and leave the results with God. If you would get the very most profit out of your Bible study resolve that from this time you will claim every clear promise and obey every plain command, and that as to the promises and commands whose import is not yet clear you will try to get their meaning made clear. (4) Studying the Bible as the Word of God involves, in the fourth place, studying it in God's presence. When you read a verse of Scripture hear the voice of the living God speaking directly to you in these written words. There is new power and attractiveness in the Bible when you have learned to hear a living, present Person, God our Father, Himself talking directly to you in these words. One of the most fascinating and inspiring statements in the Bible is, "Enoch walked with God" (Gen. 5:24). We can have God's glorious companionship any moment we please by simply opening His Word and letting the living and ever-present God speak to us through it. With what holy awe and strange and unutterable joy one studies the Bible if he studies it in this way! It is heaven come down to earth.

8. The eighth and last condition of the most profitable Bible study is prayerfulness. The Psalmist prayed, "Open thou mine eyes, that I may behold wondrous things out of thy law" (Ps. 119:18). Every one who desires to get the greatest profit out of his Bible study needs to offer that or a similar prayer every time he undertakes the study of the Word. Few keys open so many caskets that contain hidden treasure as prayer. Few clues unravel so many difficulties. Few microscopes will disclose so many beauties hidden from the eye of the ordinary observer. What new light often shines from an old familiar text as you bend over it in prayer! I believe in studying the Bible a good deal on your knees. When one reads an entire book through on his knees—and this is easily done—that book has a new meaning and becomes a new book. One ought never to open the Bible to read it without at least lifting the heart to God in silent prayer that He will interpret it, illumine its pages by the light of His Spirit. It is a rare privilege to study any book under the immediate guidance and instruction of its author, and this is the privilege of us all in study-

ing the Bible. When one comes to a passage that is difficult to understand or difficult to interpret, instead of giving it up, or rushing to some learned friend, or to some commentary, he should lay that passage before God, and ask Him to explain it to him, pleading God's promise, "If any of you lack wisdom, let him ask of God, that giveth to all men liberally, and upbraideth not, and it shall be given him. But let him ask in faith, nothing doubting" (Jas. 1:5, 6, R.V.). It is simply wonderful how the seemingly most difficult passages become plain by this treatment. Harry Morehouse, one of the most remarkable Bible scholars among unlearned men, used to say that whenever he came to a passage in the Bible which he could not understand, he would search through the Bible for some other passage that threw light on it, and lay it before God in prayer, and that he had never found a passage that did not yield to this treatment. The author of this book has had a quite similar experience. Some years ago, accompanied by a friend, I was making a tour afoot of Franconian Switzerland, and visiting some of the more famous zoolithic caves. One day a rural letter carrier stopped us and asked if we would like to see a cave of rare beauty and interest, away from the beaten tracks of travel. Of course, we said, yes. He led us through the woods and underbrush to the mouth of the cave, and we entered. All was dark and uncanny. He expatiated greatly on the beauty of the cave, telling us of altars and fantastic formations, but we could see absolutely nothing. Now and then he uttered a note to warn us to have a care, as near our feet lay a gulf the bottom of which had never been discovered. We began to fear that we might be the first discoverers of the bottom. There was nothing pleasant about the whole affair. But as soon as a magnesium taper was lighted, all became different. There were the stalagmites rising from the floor to meet the stalactites as they came down from the ceiling. There was the great altar of nature, that peasant fancy ascribed to the skill of ancient worshipers; there were the beautiful and fantastic formations on every hand, and all glistening in fairylike beauty in the brilliant light. So I have often thought it was with many a passage of Scripture. Others tell you of its beauty, but you cannot see it. It looks dark and intricate and forbidding and dangerous, but when God's own light is kindled there by prayer how different all becomes in an instant. You see a beauty that language cannot express, and that only those can appreciate who have stood there in the same light. He who would understand and love his Bible must be much in prayer. Prayer will do more than a college education to make the Bible an open and a glorious book. Perhaps the best lesson I learned in a German university, where I had the privilege of receiving the instruction of one of the most noted and most gifted Bible teachers of any age, was that which came through the statement of one who knew him that Professor Delitzsch worked out much of his teaching on his knees.

XV. The Distinctive Doctrine
of Protestantism

*Be it known unto you therefore, brethren, that through
this man is proclaimed unto you remission of sins: and by
him every one that believeth is justified from all things,
from which ye could not be justified by the law of Moses.*

ACTS 13:38, 39.

*But to him that worketh not but, believeth on him that
justifieth the ungodly, his faith is reckoned for right-
eousness.*

ROMANS 4:5.

THESE ARE two remarkable passages and this chapter will
be occupied with an exposition of them. Our subject is,
"The Distinctive Doctrine of Protestantism: Justification
by Faith." The doctrine of Justification by Faith was the
doctrine that made the Reformation. It is today one of the
cardinal doctrines of the Evangelical Faith. This doctrine,
though first fully expounded and constantly emphasized
by Paul, runs throughout the entire Bible from Genesis to
Revelation. It is in the first book of the Bible, the book of
Genesis, that we read, "Abraham believed in the Lord; and
he counted it to him for righteousness" (Gen. 15:6). In
these words in the very first book in the Bible we have the
germ of the whole gracious and precious doctrine of Jus-
tification by Faith.

1. What Is Justification?

The first thing for us to understand clearly is just what justification is. It is at this point that many go astray in their study of this great truth. There are two fundamentally different definitions of the meaning of the words "justify" and "justification." The one definition of "justify" is, to make righteous, and of "justification," being made righteous. The other definition of "justify" is, to reckon, declare, or show to be righteous, and of "justification," being declared or reckoned righteous. On these two different definitions two schools of thought depart from one another. Which is the true definition? The way to settle the meaning of any word in the Bible is by an examination of all the passages in which that word and its derivatives are found. If anyone will go through the Bible, the Old Testament and the New, and carefully study all the passages in which the word "justify" and its derivatives are found, he will discover that beyond question, in Biblical usage, to "justify" means, not to make righteous, but to reckon righteous, declare righteous, or show to be righteous. A man is justified before God when God reckons him righteous. This appears, for example, in the fourth chapter of Romans 4:2-8, R.V.: "For if Abraham was justified by works, he hath whereof to glory; but not toward God. For what saith the scripture? And Abraham believed God and it was reckoned unto him for righteousness. Now to him that worketh, the reward is not reckoned as of grace, but as of debt. But to him that worketh not, but believeth on him that justifieth the ungodly, his faith is reckoned for righteousness even as David also pronounced blessing upon the man unto whom God reckoneth righteousness apart from works, saying, Blessed are they whose iniquities are forgiven, and whose sins are covered. Blessed is the man to whom the Lord will not reckon sin." It is plain from this passage, as from many other passages, that a man is justified when God reckons him righteous, no matter what his principles of character and of conduct may have been. We shall see later that justification means more than mere forgiveness.

II. How Are Men Justified?

We come now to the second question, and the all-important question, How are men justified? In general, there are two opposing views of justification: one that men are justified by their own works, that is, on the ground of something which they do themselves. This view may be variously expressed. The good works that men speak of as a ground of their justification may be their good moral conduct, or their keeping the Golden Rule, or something of that sort. Or they may be works of religion, such as doing penance, saying prayers, joining the church, going to church, being baptized, or partaking of the Lord's Supper, or the performance of some other religious duties. But these all amount to the same thing: it is something that we ourselves do that brings justification; some works of our own, some works that we do, are taken as the ground of our justification. The other view of justification is that we are justified, not by our own works in any sense, but entirely by the work of another, that is, by the atoning death of Jesus Christ on the cross of Calvary, that our own works have nothing to do with our justification, but that we are justified entirely by Christ's finished and complete work of atonement, by His death for us on the Cross, and that all that we have to do with our justification is merely to appropriate it to ourselves by simply trusting in

Him who made the atonement. Which is the correct view? We shall go directly to the Bible for the answer to this all-important question.

1. The first part of the answer we will find in Romans 3:20, "Therefore by the deeds of the law there shall no flesh be justified in his sight: for through the law cometh the knowledge of sin." It is here very plainly stated that we are not justified by keeping the law of God, either the Mosaic law or any other law, and that the law is given, not to bring us justification, but to bring us a knowledge of sin, that is, to bring us to the realization of our need of justification by grace. It is plainly stated here that no man is justified by works of the law. The same great truth is found in Galatians 2:16: "Knowing that a man is not justified by the works of the law, save through faith in Jesus Christ, even we believed on Christ Jesus, that we might be justified by faith in Christ, and not by the works of the law: for by the works of the law shall no flesh be justified." Justification by any works of our own is an impossibility. It is an impossibility because to be justified by works of the law, or by anything we can do, we must perfectly keep the law of God. The law demands perfect obedience as a ground of justification. It says, "Cursed is every one that continueth not in all things that are written in the book of the law to do them" (Gal. 3:10). But not one of us has perfectly kept the law of God, and the moment we break the law of God at any point, justification by works becomes an absolute impossibility. So as far as the law of God is concerned, every one of us is "under the curse," and if we are justified at all we must find some way of justification other than by keeping the law of God. God did not give man the law with the expectation or intention that he would keep it and be justified thereby. He gave

man the law to produce conviction of sin, to stop men's mouths, and to lead them to Christ. Or, as Paul puts it in Romans 3:19, 20, "Now ye know that what things soever the law saith, it speaketh to them that are under the law; that every mouth may be stopped, and all the world may be brought under the judgment of God: because by the works of the law shall no flesh be justified in his sight: for through the law cometh the knowledge of sin." As plain as these words of God are, strangely enough there are many today who are preaching the law as a way of salvation. But when they so preach they are preaching a way of salvation other than that laid down in God's own Word.

2. The second part of the answer to the question as to how we are justified we find in Romans 3:24. "Being justified freely by his grace through the redemption that is in Christ Jesus." The word translated "freely" in this passage means as a free gift, and the verse tells us that men are justified as a free gift by God's grace (i.e., God's unmerited favor) through (i.e., on the ground of) the redemption that is in Christ Jesus. In other words, justification is not on the ground of any desert there is in us, not on the ground of anything that we have done, we are not justified by our own doing or by our own character. Justification is a free gift that God bestows absolutely without pay. The channel through which this free gift is bestowed is the redemption that is in Christ Jesus. We shall see later that this means through the purchase price that Christ paid for our redemption, that is, the shedding of His blood on the cross of Calvary.

3. This leads us to the third part of the answer to the question, how men are justified. We find this third part of the answer in Romans 5:9, "Much more then, being now justified by his blood, shall we be saved from the wrath

of God through him." Here we are told in so many words that we are justified, or counted righteous "by," or more literally, "in," Christ's blood," that is, on the ground of Christ's propitiatory death. We were all under the curse of the broken law of God, for we had all broken it, but by dying in our stead on the cross of Calvary "Christ redeemed us from the curse of the law, having become a curse for us; for it is written, Cursed is every one that hangeth on a tree" (Gal. 3:13). Or, as Peter puts it in I Peter 2:24, "Who his own self bare our sins in his own body on the tree." Or, as Paul puts it again in II Corinthians 5:21, "Him who knew no sin he [God] made to be sin on our behalf; that we might become the righteousness of God in him." We shall have occasion to come back to this passage later. All that I wish you to notice in it at this time is that it is on the ground of Jesus Christ becoming a substitute for us, on the ground of His taking the place we deserve on the cross that we are reckoned righteous. *The one and only ground of justification is the shed blood of Jesus Christ.* Of course, this doctrine is entirely different from the teaching of Christian Science, and entirely different from the teaching of much that is called New Theology, and entirely different from the teaching of New Thought and Theosophy, and entirely different from the teaching of Unitarianism, but it is the teaching of the Word of God. We find this same teaching clearly given by the prophet Isaiah seven hundred years before our Lord was born: "All we like sheep have gone astray; we have turned every one to his own way, and the Lord hath laid [literally, made to strike] on him [i.e., on the Lord Jesus] the iniquity of us all" (Isa. 53:6). Get this point clearly settled in your mind, that the sole but all-sufficient ground on which men are justified before God is the shed blood of Jesus Christ, offered by Jesus Christ as an atonement for our sins and accepted by God the Father as an all-sufficient atonement.

4. The fourth part of the answer to the question how men are justified we find in Romans 3:26: "For the showing, I say, of his [i.e., God's] righteousness at this present season: that he [i.e., God] might himself be just, and the justifier of him that hath faith in Jesus." Here we are taught that men are justified on the condition of faith in Jesus. If possible, Romans 4:5, makes this even more plain, "But to him that worketh not but believeth on him that justifieth the ungodly, his faith is reckoned for righteousness." Here the Holy Spirit, speaking through the Apostle Paul, tells us that to those who believe in Jesus their faith is counted for righteousness. In other words, faith makes ours the shed blood which is the ground of justification, and we are justified when we believe. All men are potentially justified by the death of Christ on the cross, but believers are actually justified by appropriating to themselves what there is of justifying value in the shed blood of Christ by simple faith in Him. In other words, the shed blood of Christ is the sole and all-sufficient ground of justification: simple faith in Jesus Christ who shed the blood is the sole condition of justification. God asks nothing else of the sinner than that he should believe on His Son, Jesus Christ, and when he does thus believe he is justified. When we believe we are justified, whether we have any works to offer or not; or, as Paul puts it in Romans 3:28, "We reckon therefore that a man is justified by faith apart from works of the law." Or, as it is put in the verse already quoted, Romans 4:5, "But to him that worketh not, but believeth on him that justifieth the ungodly, his faith is reckoned for righteousness." A man is justified entirely apart from

works of the law, that is, he is justified on condition that he believe on Jesus Christ, even though he has no works to offer as the ground on which to claim justification. When we cease to work for justification and simply "believe on him who justifieth the ungodly," that faith is reckoned to us for righteousness, and therefore we are counted righteous. The question, then, is not, have you any works to offer, but do you believe on Him who justifies the ungodly? Works have nothing to do with justification except to hinder it when we trust in them. The blood of Jesus Christ secures it, faith in Jesus Christ appropriates it. We are justified not by our works, but by His work. We are justified on the simple and single ground of His shed blood and on the simple and single condition of our faith in Him who shed the blood. So great is the pride of the natural heart that it is exceedingly difficult to hold men to this doctrine of justification by faith alone, apart from works of law. We are constantly seeking to bring in our works somewhere.

5. But we have not yet completely answered the question of how men are justified. There is another side to the truth, and if our doctrine of justification is to be complete and well balanced we must look at that other side. You will find part of this other side in Romans 10:9, 10, "If thou shalt confess with thy mouth Jesus as Lord, and shalt believe in thy heart that God raised him from the dead, thou shalt be saved; for with the heart man believeth unto righteousness; and with the mouth confession is made unto salvation." God here tells us that the faith that appropriates justification is a faith with the heart, that is, a faith that is not a mere notion, or opinion, but a faith that leads to action in accordance with that faith, and it is therefore a faith that leads to open confession with the mouth of

Jesus as our Lord. If one has some kind of faith, or what he calls faith, that does not lead him to an open confession of Christ, he has a faith that does not justify; for it is not a faith with the heart. Our Lord Jesus Christ Himself tells us that heart faith leads to open confession; for He says in Matthew 12:34, "Out of the abundance of the heart the mouth speaketh." Faith in Jesus Christ in the heart leads inevitably to a confession of Jesus as Lord with the mouth, and if you are not confessing Jesus as your Lord with your mouth you have not justifying faith and you are not justified.

6. The rest of the other side of the truth about being justified by faith, you will find in James 2:14, 18-24, R.V., "What doth it profit, my brethren, if a man say he hath faith but have not works? Can that faith save him?" We see here that a faith that a man merely says he has, but that does not lead to works in accordance with what he claims to believe, cannot justify. Now read verses 18-24:

Yea, a man will say, Thou hast faith, and I have works: show me thy faith apart from thy works, and I by my works will show thee my faith. Thou believest that God is one; thou doest well: the devils also believe and shudder. But wilt thou know, O vain man, that faith apart from works is barren? Was not Abraham our father justified by works, in that he offered up Isaac his son, upon the altar? Thou seest that faith wrought with his works, and by works was faith made perfect [i.e., in the works to which Abraham's faith led, faith had its perfect manifestation]; and the scripture was fulfilled which saith, And Abraham believed God, and it was reckoned unto him for righteousness; and he was called the friend of God. Ye see that by works a man is justified, and not only by faith.

Some see in these words a contradiction between the teaching of James and the teaching of Paul, but there is no contradiction whatever. Here James teaches us an important truth, namely, that the faith that one says he has, but which does not manifest itself in action in accordance with the faith professed, will not justify. The faith that justifies is real faith that leads to action in accordance with the truth we profess to believe. It is true that we are justified simply by faith apart from the works of the law; but it must be a real faith, otherwise it does not justify. As someone has put it, "We are justified by faith without works, but we are not justified by a faith that is without works." The faith which God sees and on which He justifies, leads inevitably to works which men can see. God saw the faith of Abraham the moment Abraham believed, and before there was any opportunity to work, and counted that faith to Abraham for righteousness. But the faith that God saw was a real faith. It led Abraham to works that all could see, works that proved the reality of his faith. The proof to us of the faith is the works, and we know that he that does not work has not justifying faith.

On the one hand, we must not lose sight of the truth which Paul emphasizes against legalism, namely, that we are justified on the single and simple condition of a real faith in Christ; and on the other hand we must not lose sight of the truth which James emphasizes against antinomianism, namely, that it is only a real faith which proves its genuineness by works that justifies. To the legalist who is seeking to do something to merit justification we must say, "Stop working and believe on Him that justifieth the ungodly" (cf. Rom. 4:5). To the antinomian, that is, to him who thinks he can live a lawless, careless, unseparated, sinful life and still be justified, who boasts that he has faith and is justified by it, but does not show his faith by his works, we must say, "What doth it profit, if a man say he have faith, but have not works? Can that faith save him? (Jas. 2:14, R.V.). We are justified by faith alone, but we are not justified by a faith that is alone, but a faith that is accompanied by works.

III. The Extent of Justification

I think we have made it plain just how one is justified, and now we come to another question, which is the extent of justification. To what extent is a man who believes in the Lord Jesus justified? This question is very plainly and wonderfully answered in Acts 13:38, 39, "Be it known unto you therefore, brethren, that through this man is proclaimed unto you remission of sins: and by him every one that believeth is justified from all things, from which he could not be justified by the law of Moses." These words very plainly declare to us that every believer in Jesus Christ is justified "from all things." In other words, the old account against the believer is all wiped out. No matter how bad and how black the account is, the moment a man believes in Jesus Christ, the account is wiped out. God has absolutely nothing which He reckons against one who believes in Jesus Christ. Even though he is still a very imperfect believer, a very young man and immature Christian, he is perfectly justified. As Paul puts it in Romans 8:1, "There is therefore now no condemnation to them that are in Christ Jesus." Or, as he puts it farther down in the chapter, verses 33, 34: "Who shall lay anything to the charge of God's elect? It is God that justifieth; who is he that shall condemn? It is Christ Jesus that died, yea rather, that was raised from the dead, who is at the right hand of God, who also maketh intercession for us." If the vilest murderer or sinner of any kind on earth should come in here this morning, and right here now, hearing the gospel of God's grace, should believe in the Lord Jesus Christ, put confidence in Him as his Saviour, and accept Him as such, surrendering to Him and confessing Him as his Lord, that moment every sin he ever committed would be blotted out and his record would be as white in God's sight as that of the purest angel in heaven. God has absolutely nothing that He reckons against the believer in Jesus Christ. But even that is not all. Paul goes even beyond this in II Corinthians 5:21, "He who knew no sin he [God] made to be sin on our behalf; that we might become the righteousness of God in him." Here we are explicitly told that the believer in Jesus Christ is made the righteousness of God in Christ. In Philippians 3:9, R.V., we are told that when one is in Christ he has a righteousness not of his own, but a "righteousness which is of God upon faith." In other words, there is an absolute interchange of positions between Christ and the justified believer. Christ took our place, the place of the curse on the cross (Gal. 3:13). He was "made to be sin on our behalf" (II Cor. 5:21). God reckoned Him a sinner and dealt with Him as a sinner, so that in the sinner's place, as He died, He cried, "My God, my God, why hast thou forsaken me?" And when we are justified we step into His place, the place of perfect acceptance before God, or, to use the exact words of Scripture, we "become the righteousness of God in him." To be justified is more than to be forgiven! Forgiveness is negative; it is putting away sin. Justification is positive; it is reckoning positive and perfect righteousness to the one justified. Jesus Christ is so united to the believer in Him that God reckons our sins to Him. The believer, on the other hand, is so united to Christ that God reckons His righteousness to us. God sees us, not as we are in ourselves, but as we are in Christ and reckons us as righteous as He is. When Christ's work in us is completed we shall be in actual fact what we are already in God's reckoning, but the moment one believes, so far as God's reckoning is concerned, he is as absolutely perfect as he ever will be. Our present standing before God is absolutely perfect, though our present state may be very imperfect. To use again the familiar verses:

> Near, so very near to God,
>   Nearer I cannot be;
> For in the person of His Son,
>   I am just as near as He.

> Dear, so very dear to God,
>   Dearer I cannot be;
> For in the person of His Son,
>   I am just as dear as He.

IV. The Time of Justification

There remains one question to consider, though we have really answered it in what has already been said, and that is, the time of justification, or when a believer is justified. When is a believer justified? This question is answered plainly in one of our texts, Acts 13:39, "And by him every one that believeth is justified from all things, from which he could not be justified by the law of Moses." What I wish you to notice particularly now in this verse is the word *is*, "Everyone that believeth is justified from all things." This answers plainly the question as to when a believer is justified. In Christ Jesus every believer in Him is justified from all things the moment he believes. The moment a man believes in Jesus Christ, that moment he becomes united to Christ, and that moment God reckons the righteousness of God to him. I repeat again, if the vilest murderer or sinner of any kind in the world should come into this room this morning while I am preaching and should here and now believe in the Lord Jesus Christ, not only would every sin he ever committed be blotted out that moment, but all the perfect righteousness of God in Christ would be put to his account, and his standing before God would be as perfect as it will be when he has been in heaven ten million years. Let me tell you of an incident. I was preaching one Sunday morning in the Moody Church in Chicago on Romans 8:1, "There is therefore now no condemnation to them that are in Christ Jesus," and in the course of my preaching I said, "If the vilest woman there is in Chicago should come into the Chicago Avenue Church this morning, and should here and now accept Jesus Christ as her Saviour, the moment she did it every sin she ever committed would be blotted out and her record would be as white in God's sight as that of the purest woman in the room." Unknown to me, one of the members of my congregation that very morning had gone down into a low den of iniquity near the river and had invited a woman who was an outcast to come and hear me preach. The woman replied, "I never go to church. Church is not for the likes of me. I would not be welcome at the church if I did go." The woman who was a saint replied, "You would be welcome at our church," which, thank God, was true. But, "No," the woman urged, "it would not do for me to go to church, church is not for the likes of me." But the woman who was a saint urged the woman who was a sinner to go. She offered to accompany her to the church, but the other said, "No, that would never do. The policemen know me and the boys on the street know me and sometimes throw stones at me, and if they saw you going up the street with me they would think you such as I am."

But the woman who was a saint had the spirit of the Master and said, "I don't care what they think of me. If you will accompany me to hear Mr. Torrey preach I will go along with you." The other woman refused. But the saved woman was so insistent that the woman who was an outcast finally said, "If you will go up the street a few steps ahead I will follow you up the street." So up La Salle Avenue they came, the woman who was a saint a few steps ahead and the woman who was a sinner a few steps behind. Block after block they came, until they reached the corner of La Salle and Chicago Avenues. The woman who was a saint entered the tower door at the corner, went up the steps, entered the church, and the woman who was a sinner followed her. On reaching the door the woman who was a sinner looked in, saw a vacant seat under the gallery in the very last row at the back, and slipped into it, and scarcely had she taken the seat when I made the remark that I have just quoted, "If the vilest woman there is in Chicago should come into the Chicago Avenue Church this morning and should here and now accept Jesus Christ as her personal Saviour, the moment she did it every sin she ever committed would be blotted out and her record would be as white in God's sight as that of the purest woman in the room." My words went floating down over the audience and dropped into the heart of the woman who was a sinner. She believed it, she believed that Jesus died for her, she believed that by the shedding of His blood she could be saved; she believed, and found pardon and peace and justification then and there. And when the meeting was over she came up the aisle to the front as I stepped down from the pulpit, tears streaming down her face, and thanked me for the blessing that she had received. And I repeat it here this morning, not knowing who may be here, not knowing what may be the secret life of any one of you who is here, not knowing what may be the sins that may be hidden in your heart, if the vilest person on earth should come into the Church of the Open Door this morning and should here and now put his trust in Jesus Christ, that moment every sin he ever committed would be blotted out and in an instant his record would be as white in God's sight, not only as that of the purest woman in the room, but as that of the purest angel in heaven, and not only that, but all the perfect righteousness of God that clothed our Lord Jesus Christ would be put to his account and he would be just as near and just as dear to God as the Lord Jesus Christ Himself is. That is the doctrine of justification by faith. Wondrous doctrine! Glorious doctrine!

XVI. The Christian Conception
of God

God is light.

I JOHN 1:5.

God is love.

I JOHN 4:8, 16.

With God all things are possible.

MATTHEW 19:26.

His understanding is infinite.

PSALM 147:5.

WE ARE to consider again today the Christian conception of God. We have seen that God is spirit, that God is a Person and that God has a personal interest and an active hand in the affairs of men today, that He sustains, governs and cares for the world He has created, and that He shapes the whole present history of the world.

I. The Infinite Perfection of God

The next thing to be noted about the Christian conception of God is that God is perfect and infinite in all His intellectual and moral attributes and in power.

1. First of all, fix your attention on our first text: "God is light." These three words form a marvelously beautiful

and overwhelmingly impressive statement of the truth. They set forth the Absolute Holiness and Perfect Wisdom of God. The words need rather to be meditated on than to be expounded. "In him is no darkness at all." That is to say, in Him is no darkness of error, no darkness of ignorance, no darkness of sin, no darkness of moral imperfection or of intellectual imperfection of any kind. The three words, "God is light," form one of the most beautiful, one of the most striking, and one of the most stupendous statements of truth that ever was penned.

2. To come to things more specific, the God of the Bible is omnipotent. This great truth comes out again and again in the Word of God. One direct statement of this great truth especially, striking because of the connection in which it is found, occurs in Jeremiah 32:17, 27: "Ah Lord Jehovah! behold, thou hast made the heaven and the earth by thy great power and outstretched arm, and there is nothing too hard for thee." Here it is Jeremiah who makes the statement, but in the 27th verse it is Jehovah Himself who says: "Behold, I am the Lord, the God of all flesh: is there anything too hard for me?"

In Job 42:2, we read these words of Job, when at last he has been brought to see and to recognize the true nature of Jehovah: "I know that thou canst do all things and that no purpose of thine can be restrained." In Matthew 19:26, our Lord Jesus says: "With God all things are possible." Taking these passages together, we are plainly taught by our Lord Himself, and by others, that God can do all things, that nothing is too hard for Him, that all things are possible with Him. In a word, that God is omnipotent. A very impressive passage setting forth this same great truth is Psalm 33:6-9: "By the word of Jehovah were the heavens made, and all the host of them by the breath of his mouth.

He gathereth the waters of the sea together as a heap: he layeth up the deeps in storehouses. Let all the earth fear Jehovah: let all the inhabitants of the world stand in awe of him. For he spake, and it was done; he commanded, and it stood fast." Here we see God by the mere utterance of His voice bringing to pass anything that He desires to be brought to pass. We find this same lofty conception of God in the very first chapter of the Bible, that chapter that so many people who imagine themselves scholarly are telling us is outgrown and not up to date, yet which contains some of the sublimest utterances that ever were written, unmatched by anything that any philosopher or scientist or platform orator is saying today. The very first words of that chapter read: "In the beginning God created the heaven and the earth" (Gen. 1:1), a description of the origin of things that has never been matched for simplicity, sublimity and profundity; and two verses farther down, in the third verse, we read: "And God said, Let there be light: and light was." These words need no comment. There is here a sublimity of thought in the setting forth of the omnipotence of God's mere word before which any truly intelligent and alert soul will stand in wonder and awe. There is nothing in poetry or in philosophical dissertation, ancient or modern, that for one moment can be put in comparison with these sublime words. Over and over again, it is brought out in the Word of God that all nature is absolutely subject to His will. For example, we see this in Psalm 107:25-29: "For he commandeth, and raiseth the stormy wind, which lifteth up the waves thereof. They mount up to the heavens, they go down again to the depths: their soul melteth away because of trouble. They reel to and fro, and stagger like a drunken man, and are at their wits' end. Then they cry unto Jehovah in their trouble, and he bringeth them out of their distresses. He maketh the storm a calm, so that the waves thereof are still." Another description of a similar character is found in Nahum 1:3-6: "Jehovah is slow to anger, and great in power, and will by no means clear the guilty: Jehovah hath his way in the whirlwind and in the storm, and the clouds are the dust of his feet. He rebuketh the sea, and maketh it dry, and drieth up all the rivers: Bashan languisheth, and Carmel and the flower of Lebanon languisheth. The mountains quake at him, and the hills melt; and the earth is upheaved at his presence, yea, the world, and all that dwell therein. Who can stand before his indignation? and who can abide in the fierceness of his anger? His wrath is poured out like fire, and the rocks are broken asunder by him." What a picture we have here of the omnipotence and awful majesty of God!

Not only is nature represented as being absolutely subject to God's will and word, but men also are represented as being absolutely subject to His will and word. For example, we read in James 4:12-15: "One only is the lawgiver and judge, even he who is able to save and to destroy: but who art thou that judgest thy neighbour? Come now, ye that say, Today or tomorrow we will go into this city, and spend a year there, and trade, and get gain: whereas ye know not what shall be on the morrow. What is your life? For ye are a vapour that appeareth for a little time, and then vanisheth away. For that ye ought to say, If the Lord will, we shall both live, and do this or that."

Happy is the man who voluntarily subjects himself to God's will and word, but whether we voluntarily subject ourselves to God's will and word or not, we are subject to His will and word whether or no. The angels also are subject to His will and word (Heb. 1:13, 14), and even Satan himself, although entirely against his own will, is absolutely subject to the will and word of God, as is evident from Job 1:12 and Job 2:6.

The exercise of God's omnipotence is limited by His own wise and holy and loving will. God can do anything, but will do only that which infinite wisdom and holiness and love dictate. This comes out, for example, in Isaiah 59:1, 2, "Behold, Jehovah's hand is not shortened, that it cannot save; neither his ear heavy, that it cannot hear: but your iniquities have separated between you and your God, and your sins have hid his face from you, that he will not hear."

3. The God of the Bible is also omniscient. In I John 3:20, we read, "God knoweth all things." Turning to the Old Testament, in Psalm 147:5, we read, "Great is our Lord, and mighty in power; his understanding is infinite." The literal translation of the last clause of this passage is, "Of his understanding there is no number." In these passages it is plainly declared that "God knoweth all things" and that "his understanding is infinite." In Job 37:16, Elihu, the messenger of God, is represented as saying that Jehovah is "perfect in knowledge." In Acts 15:18, we read, "Known unto God are all his works from the beginning of the world." The Revised Version makes a change in the translation of this verse, but this change does not alter the sense of the truth here set forth, that God knows all His works and all things from the beginning of the world. Known to Him is everything from the vastest to the minutest detail. In Psalm 147:4, we are told, "He telleth the number of the stars; he knoweth them all by name." While in Matthew 10:29, we are told that not a sparrow falls to

the ground without Him. The stars in all their stupendous magnitude and the sparrows in all their insignificance are all equally in His mind.

We are told further that everything has a part in His purpose and plan. In Acts 3:17, 18, the Apostle Peter says of the crucifixion of our Lord, the wickedest act in all the history of the human race: "And now, brethren, I wot that in ignorance ye did it, as did also your rulers. But the things which God foreshowed by the mouth of all the prophets, that his Christ should suffer, he thus fulfilled." In Acts 2:23, Peter declared on the day of Pentecost (although the crucifixion of the Lord Jesus was the wickedest act in all history) that, nevertheless, the Lord Jesus was "delivered up by the determinate council and foreknowledge of God." According to the Psalmist (Ps. 76:10), God takes the acts of the wickedest men into His plans and makes the wrath of men to praise Him, and the remainder of wrath doth He restrain. Even the present war [World War I] with all its horrors, with all its atrocities, with all its abominations and all its nameless wickednesses, was foreknown of God and taken into His own gracious plan of the ages; and He will make every event in this war, even the most shocking things designed by the vilest conspiracy of unprincipled men, utterly inhuman and beastly and devil-inspired men, work together for good to those who love God, for those who are the called according to His purpose (Rom. 8:28).

The whole plan of the ages, not merely of the centuries, but of the immeasurable ages of God, and every man's part in it, has been known to God from all eternity. This is made very clear in Ephesians 1:9-12: "Having made known unto us the mystery of his will, according to his good pleasure which he purposed in him unto a dispensation of the fullness of the times, to sum up all things in Christ, the things in the heavens, and the things upon the earth; in him, I say, in whom also we were made a heritage, having been foreordained according to the purpose of him who worketh all things after the counsel of his will; to the end that we should be to the praise of his glory, we who before hoped in Christ." And in Ephesians 3:4-9, we read:

Wherefore when ye read, ye can perceive my understanding in the mystery of Christ; which in other generations was not made known unto the sons of men, as it is now revealed unto his holy prophets and apostles in the Spirit; to wit, that the Gentiles are fellow-heirs, and fellow-members of the body, and fellow-partakers of the promise in Christ Jesus through the gospel, whereof I was made a minister, according to the gift of that grace of God which was given me according to the working of his power. Unto me, who am less than the least of all saints, was this grace given, to preach unto the Gentiles the unsearchable riches of Christ; and to make all men see what is the dispensation of the mystery which from all ages has been hid in God who created all things.

God has no after-thoughts. Everything is seen, known, purposed, and planned from the outset. Well may we exclaim: "O the depth of the riches both of the wisdom and knowledge of God! how unsearchable are his judgments, and his ways past finding out!" (Rom. 11:33). God knows from all eternity what He will do through all eternity.

4. God is also absolutely and infinitely holy. This is a point of central and fundamental importance in the Bible conception of God. It comes out in our first text: "God is light, and in him is no darkness at all." When he wrote these words John gave them as the summary of "the message which we have heard from God." (I John 1:5). In Isaiah 6:3, in the vision of Jehovah which was given to

Isaiah in the year that King Uzziah died, the "seraphim," or "burning ones," burning in their own intense holiness, are represented as standing before Jehovah with covered faces and covered feet, and constantly crying, "Holy, holy, holy, is the Lord of hosts." And in I Peter 1:16, God cries to us, "Be ye holy, for I am holy."

This thought of the infinite and awe-inspiring holiness of God pervades the entire Bible. It underlies everything in the Bible. The entire Mosaic system is built on and about this fundamental and central truth. Its system of washings; the divisions of the tabernacle; the divisions of the people into ordinary Israelites, Levites, priests and high priests, who were permitted different degrees of approach to God under strictly defined conditions; insistence on sacrifices of blood as the necessary medium of approach to God; God's directions to Moses in Exodus 3:5, to Joshua in Joshua 5:15; the punishment of Uzziah in II Chronicles 26:16-26; the strict orders to Israel in regard to approaching Sinai when Jehovah came down on it; the doom of Korah, Dathan, and Abiram in Numbers 16:1-33; and the destruction of Nadab and Abihu in Leviticus 10:1-3—all these were intended to teach, emphasize, and burn into the minds and hearts of the Israelites the fundamental truth that God is holy, unapproachably holy. The truth that God is holy is the fundamental truth of the Bible, of the Old Testament and the New Testament, of both the Jewish religion and the Christian religion. It is the pre-eminent factor in the Christian conception of God. There is no fact in the Christian conception of God that needs more to be emphasized in our day than the fact of the absolute, unqualified, and uncompromising holiness of God. That is the chief note lacking in Christian Science, Theosophy, Occultism, Buddhism, New Thought, the New Theology, and all the base but boasted cults of the day. That great truth underlies those fundamental doctrines of the Bible —the Atonement by Shed Blood, and Justification by Faith. The doctrine of the holiness of God is the keystone in the arch of Christian truth.

5. God is also love. This truth is declared in one of our texts. The words, "God is love," are found twice in the same chapter (I John 4:8, 16). This truth is essentially the same truth as that "God is light" and "God is holy," for the very essence of true holiness is love, and "light" is "love" and "love" is "light."

6. Furthermore, God is not only perfect in His intellectual and moral attributes and in power, He is also omnipresent. This thought of God comes out in both the Old Testament and the New. In Psalm 139:7-10, we read: "Whither shall I go from thy spirit? or whither shall I flee from thy presence? If I ascend up into heaven, thou art there: if I make my bed in hell, behold, thou art there. If I take the wings of the morning, and dwell in the uttermost part of the sea; even there shall thy hand lead me, and thy right hand shall hold me." There is no place where one can flee from God's presence, for God is everywhere. This great truth is set forth in a remarkable way in Jeremiah 23:23, 24, "Am I a God at hand, saith Jehovah, and not a God afar off? Can any hide himself in secret places that I shall not see him? saith Jehovah. Do not I fill heaven and earth? saith Jehovah."

We have seen that God has a local habitation, that there is a place where He exists and manifests Himself in a way in which He does not manifest Himself everywhere; but while we insist on that clearly revealed truth, we must also never lose sight of the fact that God is everywhere. We find this same truth set forth by Paul in his sermon to the

Epicurean and Stoic philosophers on Mars Hill, Acts 17:24-28: "The God that made the world, and all things therein, he, being Lord of heaven and earth, dwelleth not in temples made with hands: neither is served by men's hands as though he needed anything, seeing he himself giveth to all life and breath and all things. And he made of one every nation of men who dwell on all the face of the earth, having determined their appointed seasons, and the bounds of their habitations. For in him we live, and move, and have our being; as certain even of your own poets have said, for we are also his offspring."

From these passages we see that God is everywhere. He is in all parts of the universe and near each individual. In Him each individual lives and moves and has his being. God is in every rose and lily and blade of grass.

7. There is one other thought in the Christian conception of God that needs to be placed alongside of His omnipresence, and that is His eternity. God is eternal. His existence had no beginning and will have no ending; He always was, always is, and always shall be. God is not only everywhere present in space, He is everywhere present in time. This conception of God appears constantly in the Bible. We are told in Genesis 21:33 that Abraham called "on the name of Jehovah, the everlasting God." In Isaiah 40:28 we read this description of Jehovah: "Hast thou not known? Hast thou not heard? The everlasting God, Jehovah, the creator of the ends of the earth, fainteth not, neither is weary; there is no searching of his understanding." Here again He is called "The everlasting God." Habakkuk, 1:12, sets forth the same conception of God. He says, "Art not thou from everlasting, O Jehovah my God, mine holy one?" The Psalmist gives us the same representation of God in Psalm 90:2, 4: "Before the mountains were brought

forth, or ever thou hadst formed the earth and the world, even from everlasting to everlasting, thou art God. (4) For a thousand years in thy sight are but as yesterday when it is passed, and as a watch in the night." We have the same representation of God in Psalm 102:24-27: "I said, O my God, take me not away in the midst of my days: thy years are throughout all generations. Of old hast thou laid the foundation of the earth: and the heavens are the work of thy hands. They shall perish, but thou shalt endure: yea, all of them shall wax old like a garment; as a vesture shalt thou change them, and they shall be changed; but thou art the same, and thy years shall have no end."

The very name of God, His covenant name, Jehovah, sets forth His eternity. He is the eternal "I am," the One who is, was, and ever shall be. (Cf. Ex. 3:14, 15.)

II. There Is One God

One more fact about the Christian conception of God remains to be mentioned, and that is: There is but one God. The unity of God comes out again and again in both the Old Testament and the New. For example, we read in Deuteronomy 4:35, "Jehovah he is God. There is none else beside him." And in Deuteronomy 6:4 we read: "Hear, O Israel: Jehovah our God is one Jehovah." Turning to the New Testament in I Timothy 2:5, we read, "There is one God, one mediator also between God and man, himself man, Christ Jesus." And in Mark 12:29 our Lord Jesus Himself says, "Hear, O Israel, the Lord our God, the Lord is one."

But we must bear in mind the character of the Divine Unity. It is clearly revealed in the Bible that in this Divine Unity, in this one Godhead, there is a multiplicity of persons. This comes out in a variety of ways.

1. First of all, the Hebrew word translated "one" in these various passages denotes a compound unity, not a simple unity. (Cf. I Cor. 3:6-8; I Cor. 12:13; John 17:22, 23; Gal. 3:28.)

2. In the second place, the Old Testament word most frequently used for God is a plural noun. The Hebrew grammarians and lexicographers tried to explain this by saying that it was the *pluralis majestatis*, but the very simple explanation is that the Hebrews, in spite of their intense monotheism, used a plural name for God because there is a plurality of persons in the one Godhead.

3. More striking yet, as a proof of the plurality of persons in the one Godhead, is the fact that God Himself uses plural pronouns in speaking of Himself. For example, in the first chapter of the Bible, Genesis 1:26, we read that God said, "Let us make man in our image, after our likeness." And in Genesis 11:7, He is further recorded as saying: "Go to, let us go down, and there confound their language, that they cannot understand one another's speech." In Genesis 3:22, we read: "And Jehovah God said, Behold, man is become as one of us to know good and evil." And in that wonderful vision to which reference has already been made, in which Isaiah saw Jehovah, we read this statement of Isaiah's, 6:8: "And I heard the voice of the Lord, saying, Whom shall I send, and who will go for us? Then said I, Here am I; send me."

4. Another illustration of the plurality of persons in the one Godhead in the Old Testament conception of God is found in Zechariah 2:10, 11, where Jehovah speaks of Himself as sent by Jehovah in these words: "Sing and rejoice, O daughter of Zion; for, lo, I come, and I will dwell in the midst of thee, saith Jehovah. And many nations shall join themselves to Jehovah in that day, and shall be my people

and I will dwell in the midst of thee, and thou shalt know that Jehovah of hosts hath sent me unto thee." Here Jehovah clearly speaks of Himself as sent by Jehovah, thus clearly indicating two persons in the Deity.

5. Another indication of the plurality of persons in the Godhead in the Old Testament conception of God is found in the fact that "the Angel of Jehovah" in the Old Testament is at the same time distinguished from, and identified with, Jehovah.

6. This same thought of the plurality of persons in the one Godhead is brought out in John 1:1, where we reach the very climax of this thought. Here we are told in so many words: "In the beginning was the Word, and the Word was with God and the Word was God." When we study the Deity of Christ and the Personality and Deity of the Holy Spirit, we shall see that the Lord Jesus and the Holy Spirit are clearly designated as Divine beings and at the same time distinguished from one another, and from God the Father. So it is clear that in the Christian conception of God, while there is but one God, there is a multiplicity of persons in the one Godhead.

This conception of God runs through the whole Bible, from the first chapter of Genesis to the last chapter of Revelation. It is one of the many marvelous illustrations of the Divine unity of the Book. How wonderful is this Book, in that the unity of thought on this very profound doctrine pervades it throughout! It is a clear indication that the Bible is the Word of God. It contains a profounder philosophy than is found in any human philosophy, ancient or modern, and the only way to account for it is that God Himself is the author of this incomparable philosophy. What a wondrous God we have! How we ought to meditate on His Person! With what awe, and, at the same time, with what delight we should come into His presence and bow before Him in adoring contemplation of the wonder and beauty and majesty and glory of His being!